THE WOUNDED GENERATION

America After Vietnam

A Washington Post book
Edited by A.D. Horne

PRENTICE-HALL, INC.
Englewood Cliffs, New Jersey 07632

Book Designer: Linda Huber
Art Director: Hal Siegel

The Wounded Generation: America After Vietnam, A. D. Horne, ed.
Copyright © 1981 by The Washington Post Company
All rights reserved. No part of this book may be
reproduced in any form or by any means, except
for the inclusion of brief quotations in a review,
without permission in writing from the publisher.
Address inquiries to Prentice-Hall, Inc.,
Englewood Cliffs, N.J. 07632
Printed in the United States of America
Prentice-Hall International, Inc., London
Prentice-Hall of Australia, Pty. Ltd., Sydney
Prentice-Hall of Canada, Ltd., Toronto
Prentice-Hall of India Private Ltd., New Delhi
Prentice-Hall of Japan, Inc., Tokyo
Prentice-Hall of Southeast Asia Pt. Ltd., Singapore
Whitehall Books Limited, Wellington, New Zealand

10 9 8 7 6 5 4 3 2 1

Library of Congress Cataloging in Publication Data

Main entry under title:
The Wounded generation.
    "A Washington post book."
    1. Vietnamese Conflict, 1961-1975—United States.
2. Vietnamese Conflict, 1961-1975—Influences and results.
3. United States—Civilization—1970-   . I. Horne, A.D.
DS558.W68   959.704'33'73   81-11845
                    AACR2

ISBN 0-13-969154-5
ISBN 0-13-969147-2 {PBK.}

To the Americans who gave their lives in the
Vietnam War,
To the unknown soldier among them,
And to these men specially known to the authors:
Thomas Jay Hayes IV
Walter Neville Levy
Christopher W. Morgens
Walter Rudolph
Charles Smith

Contents

Part Three: MANY LEGACIES

Prologue

Richard Harwood

BENEATH THE HEALED SURFACE OF AMERICAN LIFE,
painful scar tissue from the Vietnam War remains. Many of the
young men who fought it still regard themselves as outcasts,
unappreciated and repudiated by their society. Many of those who
opposed the war and were spared the fighting of it have their own
troubling memories and moments of self-doubt. They constitute,
in a real sense, a fractured generation that limps uneasily toward
reconciliation of some kind. The destiny of this generation is, of
course, undetermined and in that sense this book is an incomplete
self-portrait, a first rough draft.

It grew out of a suggestion by John P. Wheeler III, one of the
contributors. He proposed early in 1980 that *The Washington Post*
should bring together some of his contemporaries to talk out their
feelings about the war and how it had affected them. The
participants included both warriors and war resisters. Their
discussion lasted the better part of a day and constitutes a major
portion of this volume. It is laced with the obscenities and
vulgarities of the military culture and with the rage and disillusionment that still afflict many of the men and women of the
Vietnam Generation. But it reflects also the strength and courage
and good sense they bring to our national life today and will bring
to it in years ahead as leaders of the Great Republic.

Why This Book

A.D. Horne

Vietnam. The word traumatized America for the better part of a decade. The war it stood for, a war Americans entered to stop what seemed a clear case of communist aggression, dragged on to become the longest we ever fought and the most divisive since the Civil War. It divided our families and generations, roiled our campuses, ended careers, broke long friendships, sent marchers into our streets and brought down a president. The way we fought it—the search-and-destroy missions, the defoliants, the body counts, the napalm, the B52 bomb craters, the air raids on Hanoi—became a series of red flags, the subject of endless debates and of deep moral anguish.

When it finally ended, there was no V-E Day, no welcome-home parade. It ended as it began, imperceptibly. The closest thing to an official end was the cease-fire agreement negotiated by Henry Kissinger in January 1973, an agreement many of us knew was simply a paper curtain hiding an unacknowledged defeat. By April 1975, when communist troops entered Saigon, there was no more denying the obvious: America had lost its first war.

For years afterward, Americans tried to forget. The word was rarely heard. The men who had fought the war, those who had survived it, had trickled home quietly and tried to pick up their lives where they had left off. What they had done in the intervening years was not something one talked about. Why revive old arguments? The politicians of course wrote their self-serving memoirs, and a few creative artists, driven men determined to come to terms with the most searing experience of their lives, tried to pierce the wall of silence with novels and movie scripts that publishers and producers said no one would pay to see. Few succeeded.

And so another generation of Americans came to maturity knowing little and caring less about what we had all gone through. And that is the reason for this book.

It is neither a denunciation of the war nor a defense of it. There have been more than enough of both. It is not even really a book about Vietnam. It is a book about America, and about a generation of Americans whose lives were—and still are being—profoundly altered by the war. It is about how we changed as a nation, in the crucible of an agonizing conflict, and about what we have learned about ourselves in the process. It is about the American future, about the future of the Vietnam generation—the Wounded Generation. It is about the way Americans now feel about this country, about ourselves and about each other. It is, finally, a book about the prospects of reconciliation between those who fought the war and those who fought to stop it, and between those on both sides and those who took no side at all.

An editor's task can often be thankless, but in this case there are more than enough thanks to go around. To Jack Wheeler, the young Washington lawyer and Vietnam veteran who proposed and organized the symposium that grew into this book. To Dick Harwood, deputy managing editor of *The Washington Post* and World War II veteran, who turned the idea into reality. To Oscar Collier, senior editor at Prentice-Hall, who had the vision to see this book in the transcript that now forms its middle part. And to the many others who have helped make this book possible, including Frank Saunders, Carol Van Horn and Jim Webb.

Part One

THE WAY IT WAS

Going After Cacciato

Tim O'Brien

THEY DID NOT KNOW EVEN THE SIMPLE THINGS: A sense of victory, or satisfaction, or necessary sacrifice. They did not know the feeling of taking a place and keeping it, securing a village and then raising the flag and calling it a victory. No sense of order or momentum. No front, no rear, no trenches laid out in neat parallels. No Patton rushing for the Rhine, no beachheads to storm and win and hold for the duration. They did not have targets. They did not have a cause. They did not know if it was a war of ideology or economics or hegemony or spite. On a given day, they did not know where they were in Quang Ngai, or how being there might influence larger outcomes. They did not know the names of most villages. They did not know which villages were critical. They did not know strategies. They did not know the terms of the war, its architecture, the rules of fair play. When they took prisoners, which was rare, they did not know the questions to ask, whether to release a suspect or beat on him. They did not know how to feel. Whether, when seeing a dead Vietnamese, to be happy or sad or relieved; whether, in times of quiet, to be apprehensive or content; whether to engage the enemy or elude him. They did not know how to feel when they saw villages burning. Revenge? Loss? Peace of mind or anguish? They did not know. They knew the old myths about Quang Ngai—tales passed down from old-timer to newcomer—but they did not know which stories to believe. Magic, mystery, ghosts and incense, whispers in the dark, strange tongues and strange smells, uncertainties never articulated in war stories, emotion squandered on ignorance. They did not know good from evil.

CHAPTER ONE

The definitive study of the demographics of the war—who served and who didn't—was published in 1978 by two former officials of President Ford's Presidential Clemency Board. Lawrence Baskir was general counsel and chief executive officer of the Clemency Board, which reviewed the cases of draft resisters and deserters, and William Strauss was director of planning and management and editor of the board's final report. This section is excerpted from the first chapter of their book, *Chance and Circumstance: The Draft, The War and The Vietnam Generation.*

The Vietnam Generation

Lawrence M. Baskir and William A. Strauss

WHEN JOHN F. KENNEDY WAS INAUGURATED ON JANUary 20, 1961, the new President told the nation and the world that "the torch has been passed to a new generation of Americans," under whose leadership America would "pay any price, bear any burden ... to assure the survival and the success of liberty." These were brave words, very well received.

This "new generation," described by Kennedy as "tempered by war, disciplined by a hard and bitter peace," consisted of World War II veterans then in their late thirties and forties. Their "best and brightest" would later steer the nation through a very different, much more controversial war in Vietnam. Yet this time it was not they who had to do the fighting. Fewer than five hundred members of this generation died in Southeast Asia, most from accidents, diseases, and other causes that had nothing to do with combat. The rest paid the taxes to finance this $165 billion venture. It was their children, the baby-boom generation—the product of an enormous jump in the birthrate between 1946 and 1953—who paid the real price of Vietnam.

THE VIETNAM GENERATION

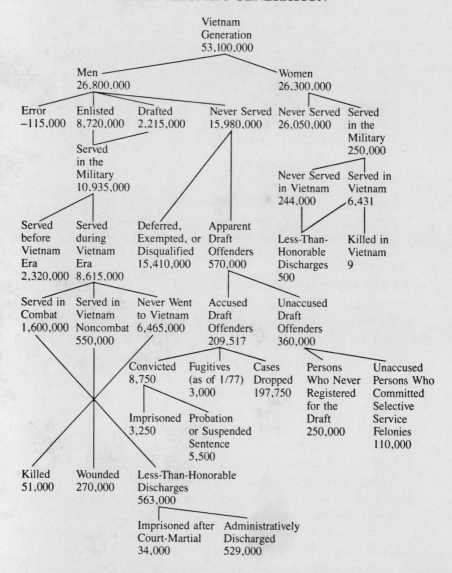

Vietnam
Generation
53,100,000

Men
26,800,000

Women
26,300,000

Error
−115,000

Enlisted
8,720,000

Drafted
2,215,000

Never Served
15,980,000

Never Served
26,050,000

Served
in the
Military
250,000

Served
in the
Military
10,935,000

Never Served
in Vietnam
244,000

Served in
Vietnam
6,431

Served
before
Vietnam
Era
2,320,000

Served
during
Vietnam
Era
8,615,000

Deferred,
Exempted, or
Disqualified
15,410,000

Apparent
Draft
Offenders
570,000

Less-Than-
Honorable
Discharges
500

Killed in
Vietnam
9

Served in
Combat
1,600,000

Served in
Vietnam
Noncombat
550,000

Never Went
to Vietnam
6,465,000

Accused
Draft
Offenders
209,517

Unaccused
Draft
Offenders
360,000

Convicted
8,750

Fugitives
(as of 1/77)
3,000

Cases
Dropped
197,750

Persons
Who Never
Registered
for the
Draft
250,000

Unaccused
Persons Who
Committed
Selective
Service
Felonies
110,000

Imprisoned
3,250

Probation
or Suspended
Sentence
5,500

Killed
51,000

Wounded
270,000

Less-Than-Honorable
Discharges
563,000

Imprisoned after
Court-Martial
34,000

Administratively
Discharged
529,000

Fifty-three million Americans came of age during the Vietnam war. Roughly half were women, immune from the draft. Only six thousand women saw military service in Vietnam, none in combat. But as sisters, girl friends, and wives, millions of draft-age women paid a heavy share of the emotional cost of the war.

For their male counterparts, the war had devastating consequences. 26,800,000 men came of draft age between August 7, 1964, when the Tonkin Gulf Resolution marked the nation's formal entry into the war, and March 29, 1973, when the last American troops left. Fifty-one thousand died—17,000 from gunshot wounds, 7,500 from multiple fragmentation wounds, 6,750 from grenades and mines, 10,500 from other enemy action, 8,000 from nonhostile causes, and 350 by suicide. Another 270,000 were wounded, 21,000 of whom were disabled. Roughly 5,000 lost one or more limbs in the war. A half million were branded as criminals, more than two million served in the war zone, and millions more had their futures shaped by the threat of going to war.

These were the sons of parents reunited after a long but victorious war, parents who, in columnist George Will's description, "were anxious to turn from the collective task of history-making to the private task of family-making. Like Studebakers and toothpaste, the next batch of children would be 'new and improved.'" Having faced depression and war, they wanted their children to know nothing but peace and prosperity. As William Manchester noted in *The Glory and the Dream*, their offspring would be "adorable as babies, cute as grade school pupils, and striking as they entered their teens. After high school they would attend the best colleges and universities in the country, where their parents would be very, very proud of them." They were the Dr. Spock generation, the Sputnik generation, the Pepsi generation, and eventually the Woodstock generation. But above all else, they became the Vietnam generation.

As children and teenagers, they had grown accustomed to the existence of the draft. Some looked forward to military service as an exciting and potentially valuable experience—a chance to demonstrate their manhood, serve their country, and get some adventure before settling down. Others saw the draft as an unpleasant but nonetheless tolerable demand on two years of their lives. Many, especially those from well-to-do families, looked upon the draft as something to avoid, an unwelcome interference with their personal plans. But most never thought much about it. Consciously or unconsciously, they put the draft out of their minds; it was something that happened to someone else, never to them.

But when the generation and the Vietnam war collided, the the draft became a preeminent concern. In 1966, a survey of high-school sophomores found that only 7 percent mentioned the draft or Vietnam as one of "the problems young men your age worry about most." But when the same question was asked of the same individuals after their high-school graduation in 1969, that number had grown to 75 percent. Few 19- to 26-year-olds were eager to risk their lives in Vietnam.

Although only 6 percent of all young men were needed to fight, the Vietnam draft cast the entire generation into a contest for individual survival. The draft was not, however, an arbitrary and omnipotent force, imposing itself like blind fate upon men who were powerless to resist. Instead, it worked as an instrument of Darwinian social policy. The "fittest"—those with background, wit, or money—managed to escape. Through an elaborate structure of deferments, exemptions, legal technicalities, and noncombat military alternatives, the draft rewarded those who manipulated the system to their advantage.

Among this generation, fighting for one's country was not a source of pride; it was misfortune. Going to Vietnam was the penalty for those who lacked the wherewithal to avoid it. A 1971 Harris survey found that most Americans believed that those who went to Vietnam were "suckers, having to risk their lives in the wrong war, in the wrong place, at the wrong time."

Much of this sentiment reflected the public's growing disen-

chantment with American involvement in Vietnam. The out-
spoken antiwar views of many young people helped sway public
opinion and turn around the nation's policies. Their activism
involved moral courage, but little concrete sacrifice. Except for
occasional individuals who, on principle, abandoned deferments
and exemptions to go to prison or take exile, opposing the war
was in every draft-age man's self-interest. The sooner the war
ended, the less likely it was that he would bear personal
hardship. . . .

"The result," as Yale University president Kingman Brew-
ster noted, was "a cynical avoidance of service, a corruption of the
aims of education, a tarnishing of the national spirit, . . . and a
cops and robbers view of national obligation." Avoiding Vietnam
became a generation-wide preoccupation. According to the Notre
Dame survey, approximately 15 million (60 percent) of the draft-
age men who did not see combat took positive steps to help fate
along. More than half of all men who escaped the draft, and
almost half of all servicemen who escaped combat, believe today
that the actions they took were wholly or partly responsible for
keeping them away from the fighting.

Avoiding Vietnam did not necessarily mean emerging unscathed. For one in four, it meant hurried marriages, unwanted
children, misdirected careers, or physical impairments. But
millions emerged untouched, triumphant in what New Orleans
draft counselor Collins Vallee called a "victory over the government." They never went to war, and they never faced the costly
alternatives of prison, exile, or court-martial.

Avoidance was available to everyone. Ghetto youths side-
stepped the draft by failing to register. High-school dropouts
married and had children. But by far the greatest number of
escape routes were open to youths from privileged backgrounds.
Through status deferments, physical exemptions, or safe enlist-
ments, they had little difficulty staying far from Vietnam. Even
doctors, who were subject to special draft calls, were seldom
involved in the war. Fewer than one of every ten medical-school

graduates was drafted; many of the rest found refuge in the National Institutes of Health, Public Health Service, or the reserves.

The draftees who fought and died in Vietnam were primarily society's "losers," the same men who get left behind in schools, jobs, and other forms of social competition. The discriminatory social, economic, and racial impact of Vietnam cannot be fairly measured against other wars in American history, but the American people were never before as conscious of how unevenly the obligation to serve was distributed. Few of the nation's elite had sons or close friends who did any fighting. Leslie Fiedler, commenting about his university community, wrote that he

> had never known a single family that had lost a son in Vietnam, or indeed, one with a son wounded, missing in action, or held prisoner of war. And this despite the fact that American casualties in Vietnam are already almost equal to those of World War I. Nor am I alone in my strange plight; in talking to friends about a subject they seem eager not to discuss, I discover they can, they must, all say the same....

The racial inequities became a major scandal of the late 1960s. General S. L. A. Marshall commented that he had seen

> too many of our battalions come out of line after hard struggle and heavy loss. In the average rifle company, the strength was 50% composed of Negroes, Southwestern Mexicans, Puerto Ricans, Guamanians, Nisei, and so on. But a real cross-section of American youth? Almost never.

At the end of World War II, blacks comprised 12 percent of all combat troops; by the start of the Vietnam war, their share had grown to 31 percent. In 1965, blacks accounted for 24 percent of all Army combat deaths. The Defense Department undertook a concerted campaign to reduce the minorities' share of the fighting. That share was reduced to 16 percent in 1966, and 13 percent in 1968. In 1970, the figure for all services was under 9 percent.

Over the course of the war, minorities did more than their share of the fighting and dying. Yet the most serious inequities were social and economic. Poorly educated, low-income whites and poorly educated, low-income blacks together bore a vastly disproportionate share of the burdens of Vietnam. The Notre Dame survey found that men from disadvantaged backgrounds were about twice as likely as their better-off peers to serve in the military, go to Vietnam, and see combat. (See the table below.) These were the men President Eisenhower once called "sitting ducks" for the draft.

LIKELIHOOD OF VIETNAM-ERA SERVICE

	Military Service	Vietnam Service	Combat Service
Low-Income	40%	19%	15%
Middle-Income	30%	12%	7%
High-Income	24%	9%	7%
High-School Dropouts	42%	18%	14%
High-School Graduates	45%	21%	17%
College Graduates	23%	12%	9%

The government did not undertake any wartime studies of the social and economic incidence of military service. The only contemporary evidence was scattered and anecdotal. A 1965-66 survey discovered that college graduates made up only 2 percent of all draftees. Congressman Alvin O'Konski took a personal survey of one hundred inductees from his northern Wisconsin district. Not one of them came from a family with an annual income of over $5,000....

After the war was over, however, the evidence began to mount. Postwar Army records showed that an enlisted man who was a college graduate had a 42 percent chance of going to Vietnam, versus a 64 percent chance for a high-school graduate and a 70 percent chance for a high-school dropout. Surveys in Long Island, Wisconsin, and Salt Lake City found a very heavy incidence of combat deaths among disadvantaged youths. In the most significant study thus far, Gilbert Badillo and David Curry analyzed casualties suffered by Chicago neighborhoods with different socioeconomic characteristics. They discovered that youths from low-income neighborhoods were three times as likely to die in Vietnam as youths from high-income neighborhoods. They also found youths from neighborhoods with low educational levels to be four times as likely to die in Vietnam as youths from better-educated neighborhoods.

During World War II, conscription and combat service were matters of personal honor. Men bent the rules to get into military service. Patriotism knew no class boundaries; Winthrop Rockefeller and the president of the New York Stock Exchange volunteered to be among the first ten thousand to submit to induction. Returning veterans were public heroes. Prisoners of war were more an embarrassment than the object of national pride. But among the tragic ironies of Vietnam, the only real heroes of the war were POWs. Ordinarily, they were not members of the younger generation; they were Air Force and Navy pilots, officers well beyond draft age. The youths returning as combat veterans were easily forgotten.

America was not winning the war, and many people were ashamed of what was happening. With the war calling into question so much of America's self-esteem, and with so many young men resisting the war, the nation needed assurance that patriotism still had meaning. Draft resisters and deserters thus became the folk villains of the times. John Geiger of the American Legion spoke for a great many Americans when he called them "a mixture of victims of error, deliberate conspirators, and professional criminals." Their detractors insisted that their numbers were small—Richard Nixon referred to them as "those few hundreds"—and that the judicial system dealt with them swiftly and severely. None of this was true, but it helped reaffirm traditional values.

The national conscience was also salved by comparing the cowardice of draft resisters and deserters with the courage of combat soldiers. This helped blind the nation to the fact that 25 million men of military age did not serve in Vietnam, and that relatively few were touched directly by the sacrifices of those who did. . . .

As important a symbol as the draft resisters and deserters have been, Americans know little about them. They are, like the draftees who saw combat, society's "losers"—disproportionately black, poorly educated youths from low-income families. Had they been better advised or more clever, most could have found one of the escape routes used by so many others. The disadvantaged not only did more than their share of the fighting; they also paid too much of the penalty for not fighting.

Vietnam-era draft and military offenders number more than a million. An estimated 570,000 men committed draft violations that could have sent them to prison for five years. Yet fewer than half were reported to federal prosecutors, only some 25,000 were indicted, and fewer than 9,000 convicted. Just 3,250 went to prison, most of whom were paroled within a year. In the military, a quarter of a million men were punished with Undesirable, Bad Conduct, or Dishonorable Discharges, branding them as deserters or military criminals of other sorts. Yet only 13 percent of them were convicted by court-martial, and even they seldom spent more than a few months in prison. Another 300,000 servicemen were sent home with General Discharges, which are technically given "under honorable conditions," although they are nonetheless a handicap in these men's search for jobs.

A great many escaped the brunt of the law because of legal or administrative problems. More than 100,000 draft cases were dismissed because of draft boards' failure to obey court-imposed rules. The overburdened military justice system gave 130,000 servicemen undesirable discharges as plea bargains, sparing the armed forces the expense of trying and imprisoning them. But, in part, this leniency reflected the views of many prosecutors, judges, and military officers that these individuals did not deserve the stiff punishments the public thought they were getting....

The opprobrium of "evader" is inappropriate for large categories of Vietnam-era offenders. About one-third of all draft resisters could have avoided the draft through deferments, exemptions, and legal loopholes, but they insisted on accepting exile or punishment as the consequence of their beliefs. One-fifth of all deserters never actually evaded Vietnam service. They finished full combat tours before running afoul of military discipline back home, often because of postcombat readjustment problems....

Until Americans evaluate the conduct of these men in the context of the entire generation's response to the war, there can never be any real understanding of the tragedy of Vietnam. The memory of the war may be too bitter for any to be cast as heroes. But perhaps the American people can begin to understand the extent to which so many young men, veterans and law breakers alike, were victims. And, with the passage of time, critics of the generation may stop setting victim against victim, fixing blame that only exacerbates the tragedy of the war.

Vietnam wrought havoc on millions of lives in a manner that most Americans may never understand. The war was, at root, the personal calamity of the generation called upon to fight it. They are the ones who faced the terrible choices, and they are the ones who suffered. "You were damned if you did go and damned if you didn't," said Ursula Diliberto, whose son was killed in Vietnam two weeks before the end of his tour. "My son was a victim, my family was a victim, all boys of draft age were victims in one way or another."

CHAPTER TWO

James Fallows' reflections on the social implications of his own (and his Harvard classmates') draft evasion, published in *The Washington Monthly* in October 1975, constitute one of the earliest and most influential attempts by a member of the Vietnam generation to think through the experiences they shared and didn't share. This is an excerpted version of that much-discussed article.

What Did You Do in the Class War, Daddy?

James Fallows

MANY PEOPLE THINK THAT THE WORST SCARS OF THE war years have healed. I don't. Vietnam has left us with a heritage rich in possibilities for class warfare, and I would like to start telling about it with this story:

In the fall of 1969, I was beginning my final year in college. As the months went by, the rock on which I had unthinkingly anchored my hopes—the certainty that the war in Vietnam would be over before I could possibly fight—began to crumble. It shattered altogether on Thanksgiving weekend when, while riding back to Boston from a visit with my relatives, I heard that the draft lottery had been held and my birthdate had come up number 45. I recognized for the first time that, inflexibly, I must either be drafted or consciously find a way to prevent it.

In the atmosphere of that time, each possible choice came equipped with barbs. To answer the call was unthinkable, not only because, in my heart, I was desperately afraid of being killed, but also because, among my friends, it was axiomatic that one should not be "complicit" in the immoral war effort. Draft resistance, the course chosen by a few noble heroes of the movement, meant going to prison or leaving the country. With much the same intensity with which I wanted to stay alive, I did not want those things either. What I wanted was to go to graduate school, to get married, and to enjoy those bright prospects I had been taught that life owed me.

I learned quickly enough that there was only one way to get what I wanted. A physical deferment would restore things to the happy state I had known during four undergraduate years. The barbed alternatives would be put off. By the impartial dictates of public policy I would be free to pursue the better side of life.

Like many of my friends whose numbers had come up wrong in the lottery, I set about securing my salvation. When I was not participating in anti-war rallies, I was poring over the Army's code of physical regulations. During the winter and early spring, seminars were held in the college common rooms. There, sympathetic medical students helped us search for disqualifying conditions that we, in our many years of good health, might have overlooked. Although, on the doctors' advice, I made a half-hearted try at fainting spells, my only real possibility was beating the height and weight regulations. My normal weight was close to the cut-off point for an "underweight" disqualification, and, with a diligence born of panic, I made sure I would have a margin. I was six-feet-one-inch tall at the time. On the morning of the draft physical I weighed 120 pounds.

Before sunrise that morning I rode the subway to the Cambridge city hall, where we had been told to gather for shipment to the examination at the Boston Navy Yard. The examinations were administered on a rotating basis, one or two days each month for each of the draft boards in the area. Virtually everyone who showed up on Cambridge day at the Navy Yard was a student from Harvard or MIT.

There was no mistaking the political temperament of our group. Many of my friends wore red arm bands and stop-the-war buttons. Most chanted the familiar words, "Ho, Ho, Ho Chi Minh/NLF is Gonna Win." One of the things we had learned from the draft counselors was that disruptive behavior at the examination was a worthwhile political goal, not only because it obstructed the smooth operation of the "criminal war machine," but also because it might impress the examiners with our undesirable character traits. As we climbed into the buses and as they rolled toward the Navy Yard, about half of the young men brought the chants to a crescendo. The rest of us sat rigid and silent, clutching x-rays and letters from our doctors at home.

Inside the Navy Yard, we were first confronted by a young sergeant from Long Beach, a former surfer boy no older than the rest of us and seemingly unaware that he had an unusual situation on his hands. He started reading out instructions for the intelligence tests when he was hooted down. He went out to collect his lieutenant, who clearly had been through a Cambridge day before. "We've got all the time in the world," he said, and let the chanting go on for two or three minutes. "When we're finished with you, you can go, and not a minute before."

From that point on the disruption became more purposeful and individual, largely confined to those whose deferment strategies were based on anti-authoritarian psychiatric traits. Twice I saw students walk up to young orderlies—whose hands were extended to receive the required cup of urine—and throw the vial in the orderlies' faces. The orderlies looked up, initially more astonished than angry, and went back to towel themselves off. Most of the rest of us trod quietly through the paces, waiting for the moment of confrontation when the final examiner would give his verdict. I had stepped on the scales at the very beginning of the examination. Desperate at seeing the orderly write down 122 pounds, I hopped back on and made sure that he lowered it to 120. I walked in a trance through the rest of the examination, until the final meeting with the fatherly physician who ruled on marginal cases such as mine. I stood there in socks and underwear, arms wrapped around me in the chilly building. I knew as I looked at the doctor's face that he understood exactly what I was doing.

"Have you ever contemplated suicide?" he asked after he finished looking over my chart. My eyes darted up to his. "Oh, suicide—yes, I've been feeling very unstable and unreliable recently." He looked at me, staring until I returned my eyes to the ground. He wrote "unqualified" on my folder, turned on his heel, and left. I was overcome by a wave of relief, which for the first time revealed to me how great my terror had been, and by the beginning of the sense of shame which remains with me to this day.

It was, initially, a generalized shame at having gotten away with my deception, but it came into sharper focus later in the day. Even as the last of the Cambridge contingent was throwing its urine and deliberately failing its color-blindness tests, buses from the next board began to arrive. These bore the boys from Chelsea, thick, dark-haired young men, the white proles of Boston. Most of them were younger than us, since they had just left high school, and it had clearly never occurred to them that there might be a way around the draft. They walked through the examination lines like so many cattle off to slaughter. I tried to avoid noticing, but the results were inescapable. While perhaps four out of five of my friends from Harvard were being deferred, just the opposite was happening to the Chelsea boys.

We returned to Cambridge that afternoon, not in government buses but as free individuals, liberated and victorious. The talk was high-spirited, but there was something close to the surface that none of us wanted to mention. We knew now who would be killed.

As other memories of the war years have faded, it is that day in the Navy Yard that will not leave my mind. The answers to the other grand questions about the war have become familiar as any catechism. Q. What were America's sins? A. The Arrogance of Power, the Isolation of the Presidency, the Burden of Colonialism, and the Failure of Technological Warfare. In the abstract, at least, we have learned those lessons. For better or worse, it will be years before we again cheer a president who talks about paying any price and bearing any burden to prop up some spurious overseas version of democracy.

We have not, however, learned the lesson of the day at the Navy Yard, or the thousands of similar scenes all across the country through all the years of the war. Five years later, two questions have yet to be faced, let alone answered. The first is why, when so many of the bright young college men opposed the war, so few were willing to resist the draft, rather than simply evade it. The second is why all the well-educated presumably humane young men, whether they opposed the war or were thinking fondly of A-bombs on Hanoi, so willingly took advantage of this most brutal form of class discrimination—what it signifies that we let the boys from Chelsea be sent off to die.

The "we" that I refer to are the mainly-white, mainly-well-educated children of mainly-comfortable parents, who are now mainly embarked on promising careers in law, medicine, business, academics. What makes them a class is that they all avoided the draft by taking one of the thinking-man's routes to escape. These included the physical deferment, by far the smartest and least painful of all; the long technical appeals through the legal jungles of the Selective Service System; the more disingenuous resorts to conscientious objector status; and, one degree further down the scale of personal inconvenience, joining the Reserves or the National Guard. I am not talking about those who, on the one hand, submitted to the draft and took their chances in the trenches, nor, on the other hand, those who paid the price of formal draft resistance or exile. . . .

First we should consider the conduct of those who opposed the war. Not everyone at Harvard felt that way, nor, I suspect, did even a majority of the people throughout the country who found painless ways to escape the draft. But I did, and most of the people I knew did, and so did the hordes we always ran into at the anti-war rallies. Yet most of us managed without difficulty to stay out of jail. The tonier sorts of anti-war literature contained grace-note references to Gandhi and Thoreau—no CO application would have been complete without them—but the practical model for our wartime conduct was our enemy LBJ, who weaseled away from the front lines during World War II.

It may be worth emphasizing why our failure to resist induction is such an important issue. Five years after Cambodia and Kent State, it is clear how the war could have lasted so long. . . . The more we guaranteed that we would end up neither in uniform nor behind bars, the more we made sure that *our* class of people would be spared the real cost of the war. . . .

The children of the bright, good parents were spared the more immediate sort of suffering that our inferiors were undergoing. And because of that, when our parents were opposed to the war, they were opposed in a bloodless, theoretical fashion, as they might be opposed to political corruption or racism in South Africa. As long as the little gold stars kept going to homes in Chelsea and the backwoods of West Virginia, the mothers of Beverly Hills and Chevy Chase and Great Neck and Belmont were not on the telephones to their congressmen, screaming *you killed my boy,* they were not writing to the President that his crazy, wrong, evil war had put their boys in prison and ruined their careers. It is clear by now that if the men of Harvard had wanted to do the very most they could to help shorten the war, they should have been drafted or imprisoned en masse.

This was not such a difficult insight, even at the time. Lyndon Johnson clearly understood it, which was the main reason why the *graduate school* deferment, that grotesque of class discrimination, lasted through the big mobilizations of the war, until the springtime of 1968. What is interesting is how little of this whole phenomenon we at Harvard pretended to understand. On the day after the graduate school deferments were snatched away from us, a day Johnson must have dreaded because it added another set of nasty enemies to his list, the Harvard *Crimson* responded with a magnificently representative editorial entitled "The Axe Falls." A few quotes convey its gist:

"The axiom that this nation's tangled Selective Service System is bound to be unfair to somebody fell with a crash on the Harvard community yesterday. The National Security Council's draft directive puts almost all college seniors and most graduate students at the head of the line for next year's draft calls. Three-fourths of the second-year law class will go off to war. . . . Yesterday's directive is a bit of careless expediency, clearly unfair to the students who would have filled the nation's graduate schools next fall."

That was it, the almost incredible level of understanding and compassion we displayed at the time—the idea that the real victims of General Hershey's villainous schemes were *the students who would have filled the nation's graduate schools next fall.* Occasionally, both in the *Crimson* and elsewhere, there were bows to the discriminatory nature of the whole 2-S deferment system and the virtues of the random lottery which Edward Kennedy, to his eternal credit, was supporting almost singlehandedly at the time. But there was no mistaking which emotions came from the heart, which principles really seemed worth fighting for.

It would be unfair to suggest that absolutely no thought was given to the long-run implications of our actions. For one thing, there were undercurrents of the sentiment that another *Crimson* writer, James Glassman, expressed in an article early in 1968. "Two years ago, Harvard students complained that the system was highly discriminatory, favoring the well off," Glassman wrote. "They called the 2-S an unfair advantage for those who could go to college." But, as the war wore on, "the altruism was forgotten. What was most important now was saving your own skin—preventing yourself from being in a position where you would have to kill a man you had no right to kill."

Moreover, a whole theoretical framework was developed to justify draft evasion. During many of the same meetings where I heard about the techniques of weight reduction, I also learned that we should think of ourselves as sand in the gears of the great war machine. During one of those counseling sessions I sat through a speech by Michael Ferber, then something of a celebrity as a co-defendant in the trial of Dr. Spock. He excited us by revealing how close we were to victory. Did we realize that the draft machine was tottering towards its ultimate breakdown? That it was hardly in better condition than old General Hershey himself? That each body we withheld from its ravenous appetite brought it that much nearer the end? Our duty, therefore, was clear: as committed opponents of the war, we had a responsibility to save ourselves from the war machine.

This argument was most reassuring, for it meant that the course of action which kept us alive and out of jail was also the politically correct decision. The boys of Chelsea were not often mentioned during these sessions: when they were, regret was expressed that they had not yet understood the correct approach to the draft. We resolved to launch political-education programs, some under the auspices of the Worker-Student Alliance, to help straighten them out. In the meantime, there was the physical to prepare for.

It does not require enormous powers of analysis to see the basic fraudulence of this argument. General Hershey was never in danger of running out of bodies, and the only thing we were denying him was the chance to put *us* in uniform. With the same x-ray vision that enabled us to see, in every Pentagon sub-clerk, in every Honeywell accountant, an embryonic war criminal, we could certainly have seen that by keeping ourselves away from both frying pan and fire we were prolonging the war and consigning the Chelsea boys to danger and death. But somehow the x-rays were deflected.

There was, I believe, one genuine concern which provided the x-ray shield and made theories like Ferber's go down more easily. It was a monstrous war, not only in its horror but in the sense that it was beyond control, and to try to fight it as individuals was folly. Even as we knew that a thousand, or ten thousand, college boys going to prison might make a difference, we knew with equal certainty that the imprisonment and ruination of any one of us would mean nothing at all. The irrational war machine would grind on as if we had never existed, and our own lives would be pointlessly spoiled. From a certain perspective, it could even seem like grandstanding, an exercise in excessive piety, to go to the trouble of resisting the draft. The one moral issue that was within our control was whether we would actually participate—whether, as Glassman put it, we would be forced to kill—and we could solve that issue as easily by getting a deferment as by passing the time in jail....

Lord Jim spent the rest of his days trying to expiate his moment of cowardice aboard the *Patna*. The contemporaries of Oliver Wendell Holmes felt permanent discomfort that Holmes, virtually alone among his peers, had volunteered to fight in the Civil War. I have neither of those feelings about Vietnam, so they are not the reason I feel it important to dredge up these hulks. Rather, the exercise can serve two purposes—to tell us about the past, and to tell us about the present.

The lesson of the past concerns the complexities of human motivation. Doubtless because the enemy we were fighting was so horrible in its effects, there was very little room for complexity or ambiguity in the anti-war campaigns. On the black and white spectrum by which we judged personal conduct, bureaucrats were criminals if they stayed inside the government and politicians cowards if they failed to vote for resolutions to end the war; the businessmen of Dow and Honeywell were craven merchants of death, and we, meanwhile, were nothing less than the insistent voice of morality, striving tirelessly to bring the country to its senses.

Of course we were right to try to stop the war. But I recall no suggestion during the sixties that it was graceless, *wrong* of us to ask the Foreign Service Officers to resign when we were not sticking our necks out at the induction center... If nothing else, a glance back at our own record might give us an extra grain of sympathy for the difficulties of bringing men to honor, let alone glory.

The implications for the present are less comforting and go back to the question asked several pages ago. The behavior of the upper classes in so deftly avoiding the war's pains is both a symptom and a partial cause of the class hatred now so busily brewing in the country.

The starting point for understanding this class hatred is the belief, resting just one layer beneath the pro forma comments about the unfortunate discrimination of the 2-S system, that there was an ultimate justice to our fates. You could not live through those years without knowing what was going on with the draft, and you could not retain your sanity with that knowledge unless you believed, at some dark layer of the moral substructure, that we were somehow getting what we deserved. A friend of mine, a former Rhodes scholar now embarked on a wonderful career in corporate law, put the point more bluntly than most when he said, "There are certain people who can do more good in a lifetime in politics or academics or medicine than by getting killed in a trench"; in one form or another, it was that belief which kept us all going. What is so significant about this statement is not the recognition of the difference in human abilities—for that, after all, has been one of the grand constants of the race—but the utter disdain for the abilities, hopes, complexities of those who have not scrambled onto the high road. The one-dimensional meritocracy of Aldous Huxley's *Brave New World* is not so many steps away from the fashion in which we were content to distribute the burden of the war. . . .

Now that the war is over, . . . the most frequently offered explanation for the neglect of the veteran is the *kind* of war we fought, and our eagerness to forget it. No doubt that is partly true. But our behavior is also shaped by *who* the veterans are. They are the boys from Chelsea, and if we were embarrassed to see them at the Navy Yard, when their suffering was only prospective, how much more must we shun them now?

Five years later, Fallows returned to the same theme in the context of President Carter's 1980 proposal to resume registration for the draft. The article excerpted below appeared in the April 1980 issue of *The Atlantic Monthly*.

HISTORY RARELY OFFERS ITSELF IN LESSONS CLEAR enough to be deciphered at a time when their message still applies. But of all the hackneyed "lessons" of Vietnam, one still applies with no reservations: that we wound ourselves gravely if we flinch from honest answers about who will serve. During the five or six years of the heaviest draft calls for Vietnam, there was the starkest class division in American military service since the days of purchased draft deferments in the Civil War. Good intentions lay at the root of many of these inequities. The college-student deferment, the various "hardship" exemptions, Robert McNamara's plan to give "disadvantaged" youngsters a chance to better themselves in the military, even General Hershey's intelligence test to determine who could remain in school—all were designed to allot American talent in the most productive way. The intent was to distinguish those who could best serve the nation with their minds from those who should offer their stout hearts and strong backs. The effect was to place the poor and the black in the trenches (and later in the coffins and the rehabilitation wards), and their "betters" in colleges or elsewhere far from the sounds of war. Ask anyone who went to college in those days how many of his classmates saw combat in Vietnam. Of my 1200 classmates at Harvard, I know of only two, one of them a veteran who joined the class late. The records show another fifty-five in the reserves, the stateside Army, or military service of some other kind. There may be more; the alumni lists are not complete. See how this compares with the Memorial Roll from a public high school in a big city or a West Virginia hill town.

For all the talk about conflict between "young" and "old" that the war caused, the lasting breach was among the young. In the protest marches on the Pentagon and the Capitol, students felt either scorn for or estrangement from the young soldiers who stood guard. What must the soldiers have felt about these, their privileged contemporaries, who taunted them so? To those who opposed the war, the ones who served were, first, animals and killers; then "suckers" who were trapped by the system, deserving pity but no respect; and finally invisible men. Their courage, discipline, and sacrifice counted for less than their collective taint for being associated with a losing war. A returned veteran might win limited redemption if he publicly recanted, like a lapsed Communist fingering his former associates before the HUAC. Otherwise, he was expected to keep his experiences to himself. Most veterans knew the honor they had earned, even as they knew better than anyone else the horror of the war. They came to resent being made to suppress those feelings by students who chose not to join them and who, having escaped the war without pain, now prefer to put the whole episode in the past. Perhaps no one traversed that era without pain, but pain of the psychic variety left arms, legs, life intact and did not impede progress in one's career. For people of my generation—I speak in the narrow sense of males between the ages of twenty-eight and thirty-six or thirty-seven—this wound will never fully heal. If you doubt that, sit two thirty-two-year-olds down together, one who served in Vietnam and one who did not, and ask them to talk about those years.

At least there was theoretical consistency between what the students of those days recommended for others and what they did themselves. Their point was that no one should go to war, starting with them. It should also be said that their objection to the war, at least in my view, was important and right. And while they—we—may have proven more effective and determined in acts of individual salvation than in anything else, they at least paid lip service to the idea of the "categorical imperative," that they should not expect others to bear a burden they considered unacceptable for themselves.

I hear little of that tone in the reaction to President Carter's muted call for resumption of draft registration. Within a week of his request in the [1980] State of the Union address, I spent time at two small colleges. At both, the sequence of questions was the same. Why is our defense so weak? When will we show the Russians our strength? *Isn't it terrible about the draft?*

Senator Kennedy, who so often decried the unfairness of the draft during Vietnam, won cheers from his college audience for his opposition to draft registration, in the same speech in which he suggested beefing up our military presence in the Persian Gulf. Kennedy did go on to argue that we should not shed blood for oil, which is more than most anti-draft groups have done to date. It would have been reassuring to hear the students say that they oppose registration *because* they oppose a military showdown in the Persian Gulf. Instead many simply say, We don't want to go. I sense that they—perhaps all of us—have come to take for granted a truth so painful that few could bear to face it during Vietnam: that there will be another class of people to do the dirty work. After seven years of the volunteer Army, we have grown accustomed to having suckers on hand.

That the volunteer Army is another class can hardly be denied. The Vietnam draft was unfair racially, economically, educationally. By every one of those measures, the volunteer Army is less representative still. Libertarians argue that military service should be a matter of choice, but the plain fact is that service in the volunteer force is too frequently dictated by economics. Army enlisted ranks E1 through E4—the privates and corporals, the cannon fodder, the ones who will fight and die— are 36 percent black now. By the Army's own projections, they will be 42 percent black in three years. When other "minorities" are taken into account, we will have, for the first time, an army whose fighting members are mainly "non-majority," or, more bluntly, a black and brown army defending a mainly white nation. The military has been an avenue of opportunity for many young blacks. They may well be first-class fighting men. They do not represent the nation.

Such a selective bearing of the burden has destructive spiritual effects in a nation based on the democratic creed. But its practical implications can be quite as grave. The effect of a fair, representative draft is to hold the public hostage to the consequences of its decisions, much as children's presence in the public schools focuses parents' attention on the quality of the schools. If citizens are willing to countenance a decision that means that *someone's* child may die, they may contemplate more deeply if there is the possibility that the child will be theirs. Indeed, I would like to extend this principle even further. Young men of nineteen are rightly suspicious of the congressmen and columnists who urge them to the fore. I wish there were a practical way to resurrect the provisions of the amended Selective Service Act of 1940, which raised the draft age to forty-four. Such a gesture might symbolize the desire to offset the historic injustice of the Vietnam draft, as well as suggest the possibility that, when a bellicose columnist recommends dispatching American forces to Pakistan, he might also realize that he could end up as a gunner in a tank.

Perhaps the absence of a World War II-scale peril makes such a proposal unrealistic; still, the columnist or congressman should have to contemplate the possibility that his son would be there, in trench or tank. Under the volunteer Army that possibility will not arise, and the lack of such a prospect can affect behavior deeply. Recall how, during Vietnam, protest grew more broad-based and respectable when the graduate school deferment was eliminated in 1968. For many families in positions of influence, the war was no longer a question of someone else's son. How much earlier would the war have ended had college students been vulnerable from the start?

Those newly concerned families were no better and no worse than other people at other times; they were responding to a normal human instinct, of the sort our political system is designed to channel toward constructive ends. It was an instinct that Richard Nixon and Henry Kissinger understood very well, as they deliberately shifted the burden of the war off draftees and finally off Americans, to free their hands to pursue their chosen course. Recall how fast protest ebbed with the coming of the volunteer Army and "Vietnamization" in the early 1970s. For this reason, the likes of Nixon and Kissinger might regard a return to the draft as a step in the wrong direction, for it would sap the resolve necessary for a strong foreign policy and introduce the weakening element of domestic dissent. At times leaders must take actions that seem heartless and unfair, and that an informed public would probably not approve. Winston Churchill let Coventry be bombed, because to sound the air-raid sirens and save its citizens would have tipped off the Germans that Britain had broken their code. But in the long run, a nation cannot sustain a policy whose consequences the public is not willing to bear. If it decides not to pay the price to defend itself, it will be defenseless. That is the risk of democracy.

CHAPTER THREE

Philip Caputo went to Vietnam as a Marine lieutenant with the first combat units that landed at Danang in 1965. His memoir, *A Rumor of War,* describes his experiences as a platoon leader in those early months of American involvement.

In Death's Grey Land

Philip Caputo

IN LATE OCTOBER AN ENEMY BATTALION ATTACKED one of our helicopter bases, inflicted fifty casualties on the company guarding it, and destroyed or damaged over forty aircraft. Two nights later, another Viet Cong battalion overran an outpost manned by eighty marines from A Company, killing twenty-two and wounding fifty more. The usual ambushes and booby traps claimed daily victims, and the medevac helicopters flew back and forth across the low, dripping skies.

The regiment's mood began to match the weather. We were a long way from the despair that afflicted American soldiers in the closing years of the war, but we had also traveled some emotional distance from the cheery confidence of eight months before. The mood was sardonic, fatalistic, and melancholy. I could hear it in our black jokes: "Hey, Bill, you're going on patrol today. If you get your legs blown off can I have your boots?" I could hear it in the songs we sang. Some were versions of maudlin country-and-western tunes like "Detroit City," the refrain of which expressed every rifleman's hope:

> *I wanna go home, I wanna go home*
> *O I wanna go home.*

Other songs were full of gallows humor. One, "A Belly-full of War," was a marching song composed by an officer in A Company.

Oh they taught me how to kill,
Then they stuck me on this hill,
I don't like it anymore.
For all the monsoon rains
Have scrambled up my brains.
I've had a belly-full of war.

Oh the sun is much too hot,
And I've caught jungle rot,
I don't like it anymore.
I'm tired and terrified,
I just want to stay alive,
I've had a belly-full of war.

So you can march upon Hanoi,
Just forget this little boy,
I don't like it anymore.
For as I lie here with a pout,
My intestines hanging out,
I've had a belly-full of war.

There was another side to the war, about which no songs were sung, no jokes made. The fighting had not only become more intense, but more vicious. Both we and the Viet Cong began to make a habit of atrocities. One of 1st Battalion's radio operators was captured by an enemy patrol, tied up, beaten with clubs, then executed. His body was found floating in the Song Tuy Loan three days after his capture, with the ropes still around his hands and feet and a bullet hole in the back of his head. Four other marines from another regiment were captured and later discovered in a common grave, also tied up with their skulls blasted open by an executioner's bullets. Led by a classmate from Quantico, a black officer named Adam Simpson, a twenty-eight-man patrol was ambushed by two hundred VC and almost annihilated. Only two marines, both seriously wounded, lived through it. There might have been more survivors had the Viet Cong not made a systematic massacre of the wounded. After springing the ambush, they went down the line of fallen marines, pumping bullets into any body that showed signs of life, including the body of my classmate. The two men who survived did so by crawling under the bodies of their dead comrades and feigning death.

We paid the enemy back, sometimes with interest. It was common knowledge that quite a few captured VC never made it to prison camps; they were reported as "shot and killed while attempting to escape." Some line companies did not even bother taking prisoners; they simply killed every VC they saw, and a number of Vietnamese who were only suspects. The latter were usually counted as enemy dead, under the unwritten rule "If he's dead and Vietnamese, he's VC."

Everything rotted and corroded quickly over there: bodies, boot leather, canvas, metal, morals. Scorched by the sun, wracked by the wind and rain of the monsoon, fighting in alien swamps and jungles, our humanity rubbed off of us as the protective bluing rubbed off the barrels of our rifles. We were fighting in the cruelest kind of conflict, a people's war. It was no orderly campaign, as in Europe, but a war for survival waged in a wilderness without rules or laws; a war in which each soldier fought for his own life and the lives of the men beside him, not caring who he killed in that personal cause or how many or in what manner and feeling only contempt for those who sought to impose on his savage struggle the mincing distinctions of civilized warfare—that code of battlefield ethics that attempted to humanize an essentially inhuman war. According to those "rules of engagement," it was morally right to shoot an unarmed Vietnamese who was running, but wrong to shoot one who was standing or walking; it was wrong to shoot an enemy prisoner at close range, but right for a sniper at long range to kill an enemy soldier who was no more able than a prisoner to defend himself; it was wrong for infantrymen to destroy a village with white-phosphorus grenades, but right for a fighter pilot to drop napalm on it. Ethics seemed to be a matter of distance and technology. You could never go wrong if you killed people at long range with sophisticated weapons. And then there was that inspiring order issued by General Greene: kill VC. In the patriotic fervor of the Kennedy years, we had asked, "What can we do for our country?" and our country answered, "Kill VC." That was the strategy, the best our best military minds could come up with: organized butchery. But organized or not, butchery was butchery, so who was to speak of rules and ethics in a war that had none?...

A helicopter assault on a hot landing zone creates emotional pressures far more intense than a conventional ground assault. It is the enclosed space, the noise, the speed, and, above all, the sense of total helplessness. There is a certain excitement to it the first time, but after that it is one of the more unpleasant experiences offered by modern war. On the ground, an infantry-man has some control over his destiny, or at least the illusion of it. In a helicopter under fire, he hasn't even the illusion. Confronted by the indifferent forces of gravity, ballistics, and machinery, he is himself pulled in several directions at once by a range of extreme, conflicting emotions. Claustrophobia plagues him in the small space: the sense of being trapped and powerless in a machine is unbearable, and yet he has to bear it. Bearing it, he begins to feel a blind fury toward the forces that have made him powerless, but he has to control his fury until he is out of the helicopter and on the ground again. He yearns to be on the ground, but the desire is countered by the danger he knows is there. Yet, he is also attracted by the danger, for he knows he can overcome his fear only by facing it. His blind rage then begins to focus on the men who are the source of the danger—and of his fear. It concentrates inside him, and through some chemistry is transformed into a fierce resolve to fight until the danger ceases to exist. But this resolve, which is sometimes called courage, cannot be separated from the fear that has aroused it. Its very measure is the measure of that fear. It is, in fact, a powerful urge not to be afraid anymore, to rid himself of fear by eliminating the source of it. This inner, emotional war produces a tension almost sexual in its intensity. It is too painful to endure for long. All a soldier can think about is the moment when he can escape his impotent confinement and release this tension. All other considerations, the rights and wrongs of what he is doing, the chances for victory or defeat in the battle, the battle's purpose or lack of it, become so absurd as to be less than irrelevant. Nothing matters except the final, critical instant when he leaps out into the violent catharsis he both seeks and dreads.

The platoon, or most of it, lay against the slope of the crescent-shaped ridge, firing into the tree line from which the Viet Cong were shooting at the helicopters landing the rest of the battalion. The tree line was about two hundred yards in front of us, across some rice paddies, the landing zone an equal distance behind. I could not remember how we had gotten to where we were, only jumping out of the helicopter into muddy water up to our waists, stumbling, heavy-legged and clumsy, with bullets lashing the air over our heads; then we had scrambled up the slippery ridge, wet and cold from the waist down, hot and sweating from the waist up. A few of my men had become disoriented in the confusion of the landing. I could see them, bunched up as they awkwardly staggered down a dike at the edge of an irrigation canal. I yelled at them to spread out, but they could not hear me. Two mortar shells gestured in the field in front of us. Two more went off behind, bursting with that ugly, crumping sound. I climbed off the high ground and ran down the dike toward the stragglers. "Spread it out, people," I yelled. "Goddamnit, spread it out. C'mon, this way. Move move *move!*" I grabbed one bewildered rifleman by the collar and shoved him off the dike into the paddy. "This way," I said. "C'mon, move. We've got incoming." Staggering like drunks, they followed me to the ridge. We climbed its reverse slope hand over hand, slipping in the sticky, drying mud. A dozen shells, crashing against the forward slope, sent up a spray of mud and singing steel splinters. We hit the deck hard. Smoke from the mortar shells rolled over the ridge, the air stinking of high-explosive. Several more rounds struck behind us. Jones, lying beside me, said, "They've got us bracketed, sir. We might just die on this fuckin' tit of a hill."

But we did not die, because the enemy did not have us bracketed. Instead, he walked the shells into the landing zone. The scene there was almost a battle portrait. The last helicopters were taking off, climbing nose down, banking sharply as they climbed, with the dark-green mountains in the background. Marines were fanning out across the rice paddies, some in extended skirmish lines, some in serried, staggered ranks, the mortar shells bursting among them. An enemy automatic rifle tack-tacked from a row of grassy mounds west of the landing zone. The bullets spurted in the light-green paddies, and one of our white-phosphorus shells flashed near a clump of palms atop one of the mounds, the orange-white streamers arcing over the graceful trees. A line of riflemen were breasting a flooded field, weapons held over their heads; they had just begun to climb onto a dike when they vanished in a cloud of shell smoke. One of the marines flew into the air, dropping sideways as he fell, the tiny stick that was his rifle sailing off in the opposite direction.

A heavy shell banged into the paddies between my platoon and the tree line. Behind us, a knot of marines were running in the crouched position men adopt under fire. Several were carrying radios, and the tall, waving antennae made an obvious target. As loudly as I could, I yelled at them to spread it out. They kept moving in a closely packed crowd, and one of my marines said, "That's battalion headquarters. Fuckin' pogues don't know enough to stay out of the rain." I hollered at them again, but they could not hear or simply ignored me. I was about to yell a third time, when they were all engulfed in smoke and clouds of pulverized earth, the shells going *crump-crump-crump* and bodies falling or flying out of the smoke. Faint with distance, the cry "Corpsman! corpsman!" drifted across the field. It was battalion headquarters, and it had almost been wiped out. The operations chief, a master sergeant with three wars behind him, lay in the muck with one of his legs blown off. The operations officer had been hit in the groin. The artillery officer had been badly wounded in the face and head. Altogether, HQ lost eight officers and a number of enlisted men. Only Colonel Hatch escaped serious injury. And the mortars kept coming in and the small arms crackling.

We heard a hollow cough, then another. Several seconds later, two 60-millimeters exploded nearby. "I heard 'em that time," a corporal said. "I heard 'em."

"Are they in the tree line? It sounded like the tree line to me."

"Good a place as any to put mortars, lieutenant, but I dunno."

I was drenched with sweat and my mouth felt as if it were full of steel wool. Battalion HQ had been nearly wiped out. D Company was suffering casualties, and ours was pinned down. My platoon was supposed to hold the ridge until ordered to do otherwise, but I felt compelled to take some sort of action. I called Neal on the radio and asked if the 4.2-inch mortar battery supporting the battalion could shell the tree line. I wasn't sure if the enemy mortars were in there—the Viet Cong were maintaining their usual invisibility—but the four-deuces would at least suppress the VC rifle fire. Neal replied that our mortars were unable to fire, and, because we were far out of range of the artillery at Danang, he had decided to call in an air strike.

The planes came in several minutes later. Three Skyhawks, flying low, streaked over us. "Bound Charley Two," the flight leader said over the radio, "this is Playboy. Mark your positions with air panels, target with willy-peter." We set out the orange, iridescent panels and fired a white-phosphorus round into the tree line. The first of the squat, dull-gray planes banked around and knifed toward that column of white smoke, Viet Cong machine-gunners firing at it wildly. Two bombs tumbled end over end from its wings. The first was a dud, but the second exploded with a blast that made the earth lurch beneath us. The platoon cheered, but the enemy mortars continued to fall in the landing zone. The second Skyhawk made a pass, dropping two more bombs into the pillar of black smoke rising from where the first had struck. One of the two-hundred-and-fifty-pounders fell on the village behind the tree line. There was a tremendous eruption of smoke, dirt, roof tiles, chunks of concrete, burning thatch, and tree branches. "Playboy, Playboy," I said, "this is Bound Charley Two. You were over on that last one. Put it in the tree line."

"Roger," the pilot answered, and I felt a giddy sense of power. I was controlling those machines.

The third plane came in, skimming the treetops, engine screeching. Two napalm canisters spun down from the Skyhawk's bomb rack into the tree line, and the plane pulled into a barrel-rolling climb as the red-orange napalm bloomed like an enormous poppy.

"Beautiful! Beautiful!" I said excitedly. "They were right on 'em."

The napalm rolled and boiled up out of the trees, dirty smoke cresting the ball of flame. The enemy mortar fire stopped. Just then, three Viet Cong broke out of the tree line. They ran one behind another down a dike, making for the cover of another tree line nearby. "Get 'em! Get those people. Kill 'em!" I yelled at my machine-gunners, firing my carbine at the running, dark-uniformed figures two hundred yards away. The gunners opened up, walking their fire toward the VC. The bullets made a line of spurts in the rice paddy, then were splattering all around the first enemy soldier, who fell to his knees. Letting out a war whoop, I swung my carbine toward the second man just as a stream of machine-gun tracers slammed into him. I saw him crumple as the first Viet Cong, still on his knees, toppled stiffly over the dike, behind which the third man had taken cover. We could see only the top of his back as he crawled behind the dike. What happened next happened very quickly, but in memory I see it happening with an agonizing slowness. It is a ballet of death between a lone, naked man and a remorseless machine. We are ranging in on the enemy soldier, but cease firing when one of the Skyhawks comes in to strafe the tree line. The nose of the plane is pointing down at a slight angle and there is an orange twinkling as it fires its mini-gun, an aerial cannon that fires explosive 20-mm bullets so rapidly that it sounds like a buzz saw. The rounds, smashing into the tree line and the rice paddy at the incredible rate of one hundred per second, raise a translucent curtain of smoke and spraying water. Through this curtain, we see the Viet Cong behind the dike sitting up with his arms outstretched, in the pose of a man beseeching God. He seems to be pleading for mercy from the screaming mass of technology that is flying no more than one hundred feet above him. But the plane swoops down on him, fires its cannon once more, and blasts him to shreds. As the plane climbs away, I look at the dead men through my binoculars. All that remains of the third Viet Cong are a few scattered piles of bloody rags.

After the fight in the landing zone, C and D Companies started to advance through the valley, driving on the blocking position B Company had set up several miles away. We slogged across the paddies beneath an unforgiving sun. There was no enemy resistance, but that did not last for long. In the midafternoon, Charley Company was ordered to search Ha Na, one of the large villages that fronted the Vu Gia River. It proved a hellish task because the village was crisscrossed by thorny hedgerows as cruel and unyielding as barbed wire fences. We had to hack through them with machetes or blow holes in them with grenades, and when we couldn't cut or blast our way through, we would circle around them, only to run into more. The result was the division of the company into small groups of confused men who bumped into each other, cursing each other as they cursed the thorns that slashed their skin and tore their uniforms.

Sergeant Pryor's squad uncovered a large cache of rice, medical supplies, and uniforms. It was stored in a poorly camouflaged pit, the rice in tins, the medical supplies in metal chests, the uniforms tied in bundles. Altogether, the food and equipment amounted to a ton. Calling Neal on the radio, I asked if we could get a helicopter to haul it out. No, he said, there wasn't time for that. The operation was running behind schedule. The company had to be at its first objective, Hill 52, by such and such a time. Get moving.

"Get moving," I said to Pryor, "we can't get a chopper."

The sergeant, his trousers in tatters, turned to me with rage on his sunburned face. "You mean leave this stuff? No way I'm going to leave this stuff for Charlie, sir. What the fuck'd they make us search this ville for?"

"All right. Destroy it in place and then get your people moving." I handed him two white-phosphorus grenades.

He threw them into the cache, which began to burn. So did a nearby house, as the chunks of bursting phosphorus landed on its thatch roof. Flames engulfed the house in a matter of seconds, and the sparks from the blaze flew into a neighboring hut, setting it afire. Four women ran out, screaming. Above their cries, I heard the team of engineers attached to the company yelling "Fire in the hole!" They had found a complex of concrete bunkers at the edge of the village and were about to blow it with TNT charges. Terrified, the women threw themselves on the ground and covered their ears as the charges went off. They screamed again when a second charge shook the ground and brought a cascade of dirt and powdered concrete down on their heads.

Sniper fire started to lash at us from the cane fields flanking the village, the crack of bullets almost indistinguishable from the sound made by the bursting bamboo frames of the burning huts. Six or seven houses were blazing now, and flames were licking at the tops of the trees. Coursey's and McKenna's platoons pushed ahead. Mine went on with the search. A corporal, his face blackened with soot, came up to me. He was holding a Vietnamese man at gunpoint.

"We found this son of a bitch trying to get away," the corporal said. "What should we do with him?"

The man, who looked to be about forty, was dressed in a khaki shirt and dark trousers. "Teach school. No VC," he said.

"I'll bet you do. Tie him up and bring him to the skipper," I said to the corporal. I did not like the look in the marine's eyes and added: "Alive. You get him to the skipper alive."

"Yes, sir," the corporal said. He pulled the man's shirt down and tied his hands with the sleeves. The schoolteacher, who turned out to be the political officer for the local Viet Cong battalion, was built like a flyweight wrestler.

"No VC. Teach school," he repeated as the marine led him away, both of them choking in the smoke.

The heat inside the village was terrific, a blast-furnace heat that seared our lungs. Pryor shoved two hysterical young women toward me.

"Lieutenant, let's take these two in. I felt their hands. They're soft. Not a callus on 'em. They sure as hell aren't peasant girls."

Before I could answer, the engineers again yelled "Fire in the hole!" We ducked down. There was another jarring blast. The girls fell, screaming and rolling in the dust. Pryor pulled them up, grabbing one in each hand, and shook them roughly. "Stop that," he said. "Stop that goddamned screaming." Then to me: "What should we do with 'em, lieutenant?"

"Let them go, for Chrissake."

"But sir..."

"*I said to let them go, sergeant.*"

He pushed the two girls away. "Yes, *sir,*" he sneered. "Yes, *sir.*" I could feel myself losing control of him and the platoon. The marines were still overwrought from the earlier fighting, and with the heat, the hedgerows, the sniping, the wailing villagers, and the noise of the spreading fire they were on the verge of losing what little emotional balance they had left.

Machine-gun and rifle fire broke out up front. Bullets were smacking into the trees around us. I learned from Neal that Coursey's platoon had opened up on a squad of Viet Cong attempting to cross the river in a boat, and enemy riflemen on the opposite side of the river, covering their comrades in the boat, had opened up on the platoon.

Several minutes later, a fighter-bomber came in to strafe the Viet Cong positions on the far side of the Vu Gia. It dove down firing rockets and cannon. Maddened by the noise, several water buffalo broke out of their pen, stampeding through the village, red-eyed and bellowing, hooking with their curved horns. One of the infuriated beasts gored a marine in Coursey's platoon and was then cut down with an automatic rifle.

Half of Ha Na was in flames by this time, the flames leaping from house to house, the fire creating its own wind. Gagging, I ran through the smoke trying to reorganize the platoon. The hedgerows and the blaze had broken it up into bands of two or three men each. "Get your people together and move on Hill 52," I said whenever I found an NCO. "Get your people together." The marines stumbled half blind through the black clouds, trying to get away from the fire. Sergeants and corporals bawled, "Get on line! Tie in on your right and left. Where's Smith's fire-team? Tie in on your right. Guide is right. Where's Baum? Baum! Where the fuck are you?" Sniper bullets whined in from the cane field.

Then D Company, three hundred yards away on our left flank, met heavy resistance. We could hear it above the sniping and the exploding bamboo, a sound like that of a huge piece of canvas being torn in half. Heavy mortars started crashing somewhere in front of us. Neal called me on the radio: Miller's company had run into a nest of enemy machine guns and had lost thirteen men. They were now pinned down and shelling the Viet Cong positions with four-deuces. C Company *had* to get to Hill 52 quickly. Get your people moving. Yes, sir. Right away, sir. "SECOND PLATOON ON LINE! MOVE!" After shouting ourselves hoarse and filling our lungs with smoke, the NCOs and I managed to form something that resembled a line. It was still a mess. Some of McKenna's men were mixed in with mine, mine with his. The platoon drove toward the hill, pressed by the fire roaring behind them, pressed by the NCOs' constant cries of "stay on line, tie in your right, guide is right." The village was a long one, sprawling beside the riverbank for a quarter of a mile. There seemed to be a hedgerow every ten yards, or a pangee trap or a ditch with crisscrossed bamboo stakes in it. There was another tearing-canvas noise in the fields beyond the canebrake. Neal again called me on the radio: D Company had advanced on the machine guns behind the mortar barrage, but the four-deuces had had no effect on the heavily reinforced VC bunkers. Miller had lost seventeen men in the assault and fallen back to call in air strikes. My platoon was not moving fast enough. We were not keeping abreast of Coursey's men.

I handed the receiver back to Jones. Yelling at the men and kicking them, I pushed them forward. Jets came in to bomb and strafe the enemy machine-gun bunkers. The planes shrieked directly over our heads, deafening us. The two-hundred-and-fifty-pound bombs made the ground tremble, and the trees and houses shimmied in front of our eyes. More planes came over, strafing with their cannon, the cannon making that buzz-saw sound. Then the first flight, circling around, flew over again and dropped more bombs. Huge columns of brown smoke jetted upward, but the VC machine guns kept hammering. "Move it out, people," the squad leaders yelled, trying to make themselves heard above the noise. "Guide is right. Don't bunch up in the center." Behind us was the advancing wall of flame from the burning village. We smashed through another hedgerow, flushed a Viet Cong from a concrete building, captured him, and then blew up the building with a satchel charge. Lunging through the sulfur-stinking smoke of the blast, dust and bits of cement raining down on them, the marines leaped into a traversed trench line. I tried to reform them there, but it was enfiladed by a sniper in the cane field. *Crack-crack-crack*. The rounds narrowly missed us, and we clambered out of the trench to pour rifle fire into the field. A Viet Cong came running out of the yellow-green cane. At a range of nearly four hundred yards, Lonehill put a bullet at the man's feet, adjusted the elevation knob of his rifle, and coolly fired again, the enemy soldier falling hard. The planes came in for another bombing run. There was a great roar, and the forms of the men in front of me blurred for an instant, as if a filmy, wavering curtain had dropped between us. While the planes bombed, we clawed our way through hedgerows and smoke toward the hill whose serene, pale-green crest we could see rising from the trees ahead. We had advanced a few hundred yards, but the hill did not look any closer. The noise of the battle was constant and maddening, as maddening as the barbed hedges and the heat of the fire raging just behind us.

Then it happened. The platoon exploded. It was a collective emotional detonation of men who had been pushed to the extremity of endurance. I lost control of them and even of myself. Desperate to get to the hill, we rampaged through the rest of the village, whooping like savages, torching thatch huts, tossing grenades into the cement houses we could not burn. In our frenzy, we crashed through the hedgerows without feeling the stabs of the thorns. We did not feel anything. We were past feeling anything for ourselves, let alone for others. We shut our ears to the cries and pleas of the villagers. One elderly man ran up to me, and, grabbing me by the front of my shirt, asked, "Tai Sao? Tai Sao?" Why? Why?

"Get out of my goddamned way," I said, pulling his hands off. I took hold of his shirt and flung him down hard, feeling as if I were watching myself in a movie. The man lay where he fell, crying, "Tai Sao? Tai Sao?" I plunged on toward the foot of the hill, now only a short distance away.

Most of the platoon had no idea of what they were doing. One marine ran up to a hut, set it ablaze, ran on, turned around, dashed through the flames and rescued a civilian inside, then ran on to set fire to the next hut. We passed through the village like a wind; by the time we started up Hill 52, there was nothing left of Ha Na but a long swath of smoldering ashes, charred tree trunks, their leaves burned off, and heaps of shattered concrete. Of all the ugly sights I saw in Vietnam, that was one of the ugliest: the sudden disintegration of my platoon from a group of disciplined soldiers into an incendiary mob.

The platoon snapped out of its madness almost immediately. Our heads cleared as soon as we escaped from the village into the clear air at the top of the hill. Miller's company, we learned, had overrun the enemy machine guns after the air strikes, but had lost a lot of men. C Company was ordered to remain on Hill 52 for the night. We started to dig in. The still-flaming rubble of Ha Na lay behind us. In the opposite direction, smoke was rising from the place where D Company had fought its battle and from the tree line the planes had bombed in the first hour of fighting.

It was quiet as we dug our foxholes, strangely quiet after five hours of combat. My platoon was a platoon again. The calm of the outer world was matched by the calm we felt inside ourselves, a calm as deep as our rage had been. There was a sweetness in that inner quietude, but the feeling would not have been possible if the village had not been destroyed. It was as though the burning of Ha Na had arisen out of some emotional necessity. It had been a catharsis, a purging of months of fear, frustration, and tension. We had relieved our own pain by inflicting it on others. But that sense of relief was inextricably mingled with guilt and shame. Being men again, we again felt human emotions. We were ashamed of what we had done and yet wondered if we had really done it. The change in us, from disciplined soldiers to unrestrained savages and back to soldiers, had been so swift and profound as to lend a dreamlike quality to the last part of the battle. Despite the evidence to the contrary, some of us had a difficult time believing that we were the ones who had caused all that destruction.

Captain Neal had no difficulty believing it. He was rightfully furious at me, and warned that I would be summarily relieved of command if anything like it happened again. I did not need the warning. I felt sick enough about it all, sick of war, sick of what the war was doing to us, sick of myself. Looking at the embers below, at the skeletons of the houses, a guilt weighed down on me as heavily as the heaviest pack I had ever carried. It was not only the senseless obliteration of Ha Na that disturbed me, but the dark, destructive emotions I had felt throughout the battle, almost from the moment the enemy mortars started to fall: urges to destroy that seemed to rise from the fear of being destroyed myself. I had enjoyed the killing of the Viet Cong who had run out of the tree line. Strangest of all had been that sensation of watching myself in a movie. One part of me was doing something while the other part watched from a distance, shocked by the things it saw, yet powerless to stop them from happening.

I could analyze myself all I wanted, but the fact was we had needlessly destroyed the homes of perhaps two hundred people. All the analysis in the world would not make a new village rise from the ashes. It could not answer the question that kept repeating itself in my mind nor lighten the burden of my guilt. The usual arguments and rationalizations did not help, either. Yes, the village had obviously been under enemy control; it had been a VC supply dump as much as it had been a village. Yes, burning the cache was a legitimate act of war and the fire resulting from it had been accidental. Yes, the later deliberate destruction had been committed by men *in extremis;* war was a state of extremes, and men often did extreme things in it. But none of that conventional wisdom relieved my guilt or answered the question: "Tai Sao?" Why?

CHAPTER FOUR

In his first book, *If I Die in a Combat Zone*, Tim O'Brien wrote about his life as a draftee serving in an Army platoon in Vietnam's I Corps area. His novel *Going After Cacciato* transmuted that experience into a surrealistic narrative that won the National Book Award for fiction in 1979. This is an excerpt.

Landing Zone Bravo

Tim O'Brien

THEY SAT IN TWO FACING ROWS. STINK HARRIS KEPT clicking his teeth. Next to him, Eddie Lazzutti moved his neck on his shoulders as if loosening up for a race. Oscar Johnson was sweating. Rudy Chassler smiled. Vaught and Cacciato were sharing a Coke, and, down the aisle, Jim Pederson sat with his eyes closed, holding his stomach with both hands. Flying scared him more than the war.

There was a long floating feeling as the Chinook fell. It dropped a hundred feet, rose, bounced, and cold air shot through the open tail section. Private First Class Paul Berlin could not understand how it could be so cold. He didn't like it. The smells were greasy and mechanical. On both sides of the ship, the door gunners sprayed down a drone of fire that blended with the chop of the rotor blades and engine, and whenever there was a slight change in the mix of sounds, the soldiers would jerk their heads and look for the source. Some of them grinned. Buff bit his nails, and Bernie Lynn coughed, but nobody said much. Mostly they watched their weapons or their boots or the eyes of the men opposite. Oscar Johnson sweated silver and Stink's teeth kept rapping together. Buff studied his right thumbnail. He would bite it, then look at it, then bite it again. Pederson, who hated noise and machines and heights, but who was otherwise a fine soldier, held tight to his stomach and pressed his thighs together. The others tried not to look at him. Cold air swept in as the ship dropped again, and Private First Class Paul Berlin hugged himself.

The door gunners squatted behind their guns and fired and fired.

They were not going down smoothly. The ship fell hard, braked, dropped again, bounced, and Paul Berlin shivered and held to the wall webbing, wondering how it could be so cold.

He tried to think better thoughts. He watched the door gunners do their steady work, hunched over their guns and swiveling and firing in long sweeping patterns, their mouths open, arms and shoulders jiggling with the rhythm, eyes dark under sunglasses and helmets. Spent shells clattered to the floor, rolling into piles as the Chinook banked and maneuvered down.

Paul Berlin rubbed himself against the cold. He watched the others. Buff was working on his left thumbnail and Bernie Lynn played with his pant leg. Pederson was curled inside himself. His eyes were closed and his tongue sometimes fluttered out to lick away sweat. Doc Peret sat next to him, and next to Doc was Buff, and next to Buff was Ben Nystrom. The lieutenant sat on the floor, leaning low and wiping dust from his rifle, his lips moving as if talking to it.

The door gunners leaned into their guns and fired and fired.

It was a bad feeling. The cold wasn't right, and Paul Berlin wondered if the others felt it too. He couldn't help watching them—all the faces composed in different ways, some calm and sure, others puzzled-looking. It was hard to tell. None of the faces told much, and the door gunners did not have faces.

The Chinook began to slide eastward, going slower now, then again it dropped sharply. Pederson's helmet popped up while his head went down, and the helmet seemed to float high a long time before falling to the floor. Pederson didn't reach for it. He kept licking his lips. It wasn't his fault or the church's fault that he feared heights; it wasn't a fault of faith.

"Four minutes," the crew chief shouted. He was a fat man in sunglasses. He moved up the aisle, rolled down the rear ramp and leaned out for a look. "Four minutes," he shouted, and held up four fingers, and then took a copy of *Newsweek* from his pocket and sat down to read.

Oscar Johnson lit up a joint.

The gunners kept firing. The Chinook trembled as the engines and blades worked harder now.

Oscar inhaled and closed his eyes and passed the joint down the row. The soldiers focused on it, watching its passage from mouth to mouth. When it reached the end of the far row, Harold Murphy got up and handed it to Vaught, and it came down the second row to Paul Berlin, who pinched the tiny roach and held it close to his lips, not touching, careful not to burn himself.

He drew the smoke deep and held it and tried to think good thoughts. He felt the Chinook falling. Pederson's face was waxy, and the cold swept in, and the gunners kept firing and firing.

The crew chief held up three fingers.

Immediately there was a new sound. The cords of exposed control wires that ran along the ceiling jerked and whined, and the ship banked hard, and Vaught started giggling. Doc Peret told him to hush up, but Vaught kept giggling, and the ship seemed to roll out from beneath them.

Working their guns left to right to left, the gunners kept firing.

"Two minutes," the crew chief shouted. Very carefully, he folded the magazine and put it in his pocket and held two fingers over his head.

The gunners leaned into their big guns, fused to them, shoulders twitching, firing with the steady sweeping motions of a machine.

The crew chief was shouting again.

The Chinook turned in a long banking movement, and for a moment Paul Berlin saw the outline of the mountains to the west, then the bland flatness of the paddies below. The ship steadied and the crew chief leaned out for another look. He shouted and held up both thumbs. Across the aisle the men were loading up. Oscar wiped his face and grinned. The lieutenant was still wiping his rifle, leaning close to it and whispering. Cold air shot through

the hull and the gunners kept firing. Shivering, Paul Berlin patted
along his chest until he found the bandolier. He pulled out a clip
and shoved it into his rifle until it clicked, then he released the
bolt and listened to be sure the first round entered the chamber.
He just wished it weren't so cold, that was all. He didn't like the
awful cold.

"Going in," the chief shouted. The fat under his chin was
jiggling. "She's hot, kiddies. Everybody off fast, no dilly-dally
shit."

He held up his thumbs and the men stood up and began
shuffling toward the rear. They grinned and coughed and blinked.
Buff balanced the machine gun on his shoulder, chewing on his
cuticles now, going systematically over each finger, changing the
gun to his other shoulder. It was hard to stand straight. The
Chinook was bucking, and the men held to one another as they
pressed toward the ramp.

"One minute," the chief shouted.

Then there were new sounds. Like dog whistles, high-
pitched and sharp. Vaught was suddenly shouting, and Eddie and
Stink were jumping up and down and pushing toward the rear.
Harold Murphy fell. He lay there, a big guy, smiling and shaking
his head, but he couldn't get up. He just lay there, shaking his
head. Holes opened in the hull, then more holes, and the wind
sucked through the holes, and Vaught was shouting. A long tear
opened in the floor, then a corresponding tear in the ceiling above,
and the wind howled in all around. Instant white light shot
through the holes and exited through opposite holes. Bits of dust
played in the light. There was a burning smell—metal and hot
machinery and the gunners' guns. Harold Murphy was still on the
floor, smiling and shaking his head and trying to get up, but he
couldn't do it. He'd get to his knees, and press, and almost make
it, but not quite, and he'd fall and shake his head and smile and
try again. Pederson's eyes were closed. He held his stomach and
sat still. He was the only one still sitting.

The gunners fired and fired. They fired at everything. They
were wrapped around their guns.

"Zero-five-zero," the crew chief shouted.

Then there was more wind. The chief's magazine fell and the new wind snatched it away. "Damn!" the chief screamed.

The Chinook bucked hard, throwing the men against the walls, then a gnashing, ripping, tearing, searing noise—hot metal—then blue smoke everywhere, then a force that drove the men against the walls and pinned them there, then a fierce pressure, then new holes and new wind, and the gunners squatted behind their big guns and fired and fired and fired. Murphy was on the floor. Cacciato's empty Coke can clattered out the open tail section, where it hung for a moment then was yanked away. Pederson sat quietly. A gash opened in the ceiling, and the crew chief was screaming, and Harold Murphy kept smiling and shaking his head and trying to get up, and the gunners kept firing.

The chief's fat face was green. He pushed the men toward the ramp.

Pederson just sat there. The chief screamed at him, but Pederson was holding himself together, squeezing his stomach tight and pressing.

"Zero-one-zero," the chief screamed. "Pull that fuckin kid off! Somebody—"

The Chinook touched down softly.

The gunners kept firing. They hunched over their hot guns and fired and fired. They fired blindly and without aim.

"Out!" the chief was screaming, shoving the first soldiers down the ramp, and the gunners went mad with the firing, firing at everything, speechless behind their guns, and the crew chief screamed and shoved.

Stink Harris went first. Then Oscar Johnson and the lieutenant and Doc Peret. They sank in the mush, but the gunners kept firing. Next came Buff, and then Eddie Lazzutti and Vaught. The paddies bubbled with the fire. Wading in the slush, falling, the men bent low and tried to run, and the gunners swayed with their firing, and the paddies were foam. Next came Harold Murphy, stumbling down, and then Ben Nystrom, and then Paul Berlin and Cacciato. The cold was gone. Now there was only the sun and the paddies and the endless firing, and Paul Berlin slipped and went down in the muck, struggled for a moment, and then lay quietly and watched as the gunners kept firing and firing, automatically, firing and firing. They would not stop. They cradled their white guns and fired and fired and fired.

The Chinook hovered, shaking, making froth in the paddies. Screaming, the crew chief dragged Pederson to the ramp and threw him out.

The gunners swung their fire in long brilliant arcs like blown rain. Pederson paused a moment, as if searching for balance in the muck, then he began wading with his eyes closed. He'd lost his helmet. Behind him, the gunners strafed the paddies, red tracers and white light, molded to their guns, part of the machinery, firing and firing, and Pederson was shot first in the legs.

But the gunners did not stop. They fired in sweeping, methodical rows. The barrels were white. Smoke hid the gunners' faces, but they kept firing, and Pederson was shot again in the legs and groin.

Slowly, calmly, he lay back in the slush.

He did not go crazy at being shot. He was calm. Holding his stomach together, he let himself sink, partly floating and partly sitting. But the gunners kept firing, and he was shot again, and this time it yanked him backward and he splashed down.

The big Chinook roared. It rose and turned, shaking, and began to climb. Clumps of rice bent double in the wind, and still the gunners fired, blind behind their sunglasses, bracing their guns to keep the fire smooth and level and constant. Their arms were black.

Pederson lay on his back. For a time he was rigid holding himself, but then he relaxed.

Moving slowly, lazily, he raised his rifle.

He aimed carefully. The Chinook climbed and turned, and the gunners kept firing, but Pederson took his time, tracking and aiming without panic.

He squeezed off a single shot. The sound was different—hard and sharp and emphatic and pointed. He fired again, then again, carefully, and chunks of green plastic jumped off the Chinook's fat belly.

The gunners went berserk with their firing, and Pederson was shot again, but still he took great care, aiming and firing and tracking the climbing ship. One shot at a time, precisely and carefully. Bobbing in the slime, he tracked the Chinook and fired into its great underside. He rolled to follow the climbing machine, aiming, taking his time. Suddenly the door gunners were gone, but even without them their hot guns kept swiveling and firing, automatically, and the Chinook trembled as Pederson calmly aimed and fired into its plastic belly.

The Chinook's shadow passed right over him.

And the shadow shrank, and soon the Chinook was high and far away and gone, leaving the paddy soapy with waves and froth, but even then Paul Berlin could hear the ship's guns.

CHAPTER FIVE

Michael Herr was virtually unknown when he went to Vietnam in 1967 for *Esquire* magazine. His *Esquire* articles soon changed that. They focused on the absurdities of the war as seen from ground level: soldiers spaced out on drugs and hard rock, wasted acts of heroism, the Saigon black market, the siege of Khe Sanh. The two excerpts that follow are from *Dispatches*, the book based on the *Esquire* pieces.

Vietnam Nights

Michael Herr

THERE WERE TIMES DURING THE NIGHT WHEN ALL the jungle sounds would stop at once. There was no dwindling down or fading away, it was all gone in a single instant as though some signal had been transmitted out to the life: bats, birds, snakes, monkeys, insects, picking up on a frequency that a thousand years in the jungle might condition you to receive, but leaving you as it was to wonder what you weren't hearing now, straining for any sound, one piece of information. I had heard it before in other jungles, the Amazon and the Philippines, but those jungles were "secure," there wasn't much chance that hundreds of Viet Cong were coming and going, moving and waiting, living out there just to do you harm. The thought of that one could turn any sudden silence into a space that you'd fill with everything you thought was quiet in you, it could even put you on the approach to clairaudience. You thought you heard impossible things: damp roots breathing, fruit sweating, fervid bug action, the heartbeat of tiny animals.

You could sustain that sensitivity for a long time, either until the babbling and chittering and shrieking of the jungle had started up again, or until something familiar brought you out of it, a helicopter flying around above your canopy or the strangely reassuring sound next to you of one going into the chamber. Once we heard a really frightening thing blaring down from a Psyops

soundship broadcasting the sound of a baby crying. You wouldn't
have wanted to hear that during daylight, let alone at night when
the volume and distortion came down through two or three layers
of cover and froze us all in place for a moment. And there wasn't
much release in the pitched hysteria of the message that followed,
hyper-Vietnamese like an icepick in the ear, something like,
"Friendly Baby, GVN Baby, Don't Let This Happen to *Your*
Baby, Resist the Viet Cong Today!"

Sometimes you'd get so tired that you'd forget where you
were and sleep the way you hadn't slept since you were a child. I
know that a lot of people there never got up from that kind of
sleep; some called them lucky (Never knew what hit him), some
called them fucked (If he'd been on the stick...), but that was
worse than academic, everyone's death got talked about, it was a
way of constantly touching and turning the odds, and real sleep
was at a premium. (I met a ranger-recondo who could go to sleep
just like that, say "Guess I'll get some," close his eyes and be
there, day or night, sitting or lying down, sleeping through some
things but not others; a loud radio or a 105 firing outside the tent
wouldn't wake him, but a rustle in the bushes fifty feet away
would, or a stopped generator.) Mostly what you had was on the
agitated side of half-sleep, you thought you were sleeping but you
were really just waiting. Night sweats, harsh functionings of
consciousness, drifting in and out of your head, pinned to a
canvas cot somewhere, looking up at a strange ceiling or out
through a tent flap at the glimmering night sky of a combat zone.
Or dozing and waking under mosquito netting in a mess of slick
sweat, gagging for air that wasn't 99 percent moisture, one clean
breath to dry-sluice your anxiety and the backwater smell of your
own body. But all you got and all there was were misty clots of air
that corroded your appetite and burned your eyes and made your
cigarettes taste like swollen insects rolled up and smoked alive,
crackling and wet. There were spots in the jungle where you had
to have a cigarette going all the time, whether you smoked or not,

just to keep the mosquitoes from swarming into your mouth. War under water, swamp fever and instant involuntary weight control, malarias that could burn you out and cave you in, put you into twenty-three hours of sleep a day without giving you a minute of rest, leaving you there to listen to the trance music that they said came in with terminal brain funk. ("Take your pills, baby," a medic in Can Tho told me. "Big orange ones every week, little white ones every day, and don't miss a day whatever you do. They got strains over here that could waste a heavyset fella like you in a week.") Sometimes you couldn't live with the terms any longer and headed for air-conditioners in Danang and Saigon. And sometimes the only reason you didn't panic was that you didn't have the energy.

Every day people were dying there because of some small detail that they couldn't be bothered to observe. Imagine being too tired to snap a flak jacket closed, too tired to clean your rifle, too tired to guard a light, too tired to deal with the half-inch margins of safety that moving through the war often demanded, just too tired to give a fuck and then dying behind that exhaustion. There were times when the whole war itself seemed tapped of its vitality: epic enervation, the machine running half-assed and depressed, fueled on the watery residue of last year's war-making energy. Entire divisions would function in a bad dream state, acting out a weird set of moves without any connection to their source. Once I talked for maybe five minutes with a sergeant who had just brought his squad in from a long patrol before I realized that the dopey-dummy film over his eyes and the fly abstraction of his words were coming from deep sleep. He was standing there at the bar of the NCO club with his eyes open and a beer in his hand, responding to some dream conversation far inside his head. It really gave me the creeps—this was the second day of the Tet Offensive, our installation was more or less surrounded, the only secure road out of there was littered with dead Vietnamese, information was scarce and I was pretty touchy and tired myself—and for a second I imagined that I was talking to a dead man. When I told him about it later he just laughed and said, "Shit, that's nothing. I do that all the time."

The second excerpt that follows is from Herr's famous description of the 1968 siege of Khe Sanh.

SOMETIMES YOU'D STEP FROM THE BUNKER, ALL sense of time passing having left you, and find it dark out. The far side of the hills around the bowl of the base was glimmering, but you could never see the source of the light, and it had the look of a city at night approached from a great distance. Flares were dropping everywhere around the fringes of the perimeter, laying a dead white light on the high ground rising from the piedmont. There would be dozens of them at once sometimes, trailing an intense smoke, dropping white-hot sparks, and it seemed as though anything caught in their range would be made still, like figures in a game of living statues. There would be the muted rush of illumination rounds, fired from 60-mm. mortars inside the wire, dropping magnesium-brilliant above the NVA trenches for a few seconds, outlining the gaunt, flat spread of the mahogany trees, giving the landscape a ghastly clarity and dying out. You could watch mortar bursts, orange and gray-smoking, over the tops of trees three and four kilometers away, and the heavier shelling from support bases farther east along the DMZ, from Camp Carroll and the Rockpile, directed against suspected troop movements or NVA rocket and mortar positions. Once in a while—I guess I saw it happen three or four times in all—there would be a secondary explosion, a direct hit on a supply of NVA ammunition. And at night it was beautiful. Even the incoming was beautiful at night, beautiful and deeply dreadful.

I remembered the way a Phantom pilot had talked about how beautiful the surface-to-air missiles looked as they drifted up toward his plane to kill him, and remembered myself how lovely .50-caliber tracers could be, coming at you as you flew at night in a helicopter, how slow and graceful, arching up easily, a dream, so remote from anything that could harm you. It could make you feel a total serenity, an elevation that put you above death, but that never lasted very long. One hit anywhere in the chopper would bring you back, bitten lips, white knuckles and all, and then you knew where you were. It was different with the incoming at Khe Sanh. You didn't get to watch the shells very often. You knew if you heard one, the first one, that you were safe, or at least saved. If you were still standing up and looking after that, you deserved anything that happened to you.

Nights were when the air and artillery strikes were heaviest, because that was when we knew that the NVA was above ground and moving. At night you could lie out on some sandbags and watch the C-47's mounted with Vulcans doing their work. The C-47 was a standard prop flareship, but many of them carried .20- and .762-mm. guns on their doors, Mike-Mikes that could fire out 300 rounds per second, Gatling style, "a round in every square inch of a football field in less than a minute," as the handouts said. They used to call it Puff the Magic Dragon, but the Marines knew better: they named it Spooky. Every fifth round fired was a tracer, and when Spooky was working, everything stopped while that solid stream of violent red poured down out of the black sky. If you watched from a great distance, the stream would seem to dry up between bursts, vanishing slowly from air to ground like a comet tail, the sound of the guns disappearing too, a few seconds later. If you watched at a close range, you couldn't believe that anyone would have the courage to deal with that night after night, week after week, and you cultivated a respect for the Viet Cong and NVA who had crouched under it every night now for months. It was awesome, worse than anything the Lord had ever put down on Egypt, and at night, you'd hear the Marines talking, watching it, yelling, "Get some!" until they grew quiet and someone would say. "Spooky understands." The nights were very beautiful. Night was when you really had the least to fear and feared the most. You could go through some very bad numbers at night.

Because, really, what a choice there was; what a prodigy of things to be afraid of! The moment that you understood this, really understood it, you lost your anxiety instantly. Anxiety was a luxury, a joke you had no room for once you knew the variety of deaths and mutilations the war offered. Some feared head wounds, some dreaded chest wounds or stomach wounds, everyone feared the wound of wounds, the Wound. Guys would pray and pray—Just you and me, God. Right?—offer anything, if only they could be spared that: Take my legs, take my hands, take my eyes, take my fucking *life*, You Bastard, but please, please, please, don't take *those*.

CHAPTER SIX

James Webb's novel, *Fields of Fire,* follows a Marine
platoon through months of patrols, skirmishes and battles in
an area the Marines call the Arizona Territory. By the end of
the book, most of the Marines have been killed. One of the
few survivors is an enlistee from Harvard, Will Goodrich,
derisively nicknamed Senator.

Fields of Fire

James Webb

THE CONCERTINA GATE CRACKED OPEN, THEN
latched quickly shut, locking them out. They walked lonely,
naked in the moon-dark, through the narrow break the road made
in the field of jagged wire. Artillery boomed behind them, six
howitzers firing far into the Arizona. The rounds crunched distant
like a futile, muffled anger. Flares hung over Dai Loc, far to the
front, like streetlights scattered on a placid hill. Just below, the
river glimmered from the flares, narrow streaks of white across it.
They moved heavily, bent like old men under flak jackets and
helmets and weapons and ammunition. Two LAAWs apiece, five
grenades, three bandoleers of ammo.

Speedy humped an extra twenty-five pounds: the radio. He
whispered into the handset. "Three Charlie, leaving the wire."

They followed the outer wire, paralleling the finger that
made the top part of the J. Back in the compound an 81-millimeter
mortar mission fired. Tubes thunked and flashed behind them.
Rounds landed like firing pistons far to the east, their front, in the
Cu Bans.

They reached the point and broke away from the wire,
seeking the streambed that would be their sanctuary for the night.
It hid beneath waves of dry, scraping sawgrass that played their
trouser legs like coarse violins as they fought it. The treeline grew
in front of them, just visible below the blackening sky.

Finally the sawgrass dipped. Streambed. The treeline loomed now, a wall of puffy dark things, wide and impenetrable. Even from this distance, seventy meters, it emanated an ashy, dead odor of burnt-out hootches. They settled quickly into the streambed, knowing its contours: this was the third time Speedy's team had worked the listening post. Each man spread a poncho liner over the abrasive grass and lay inside the streambed.

Speedy whispered to the hissing handset: "Three Charlie, all set in."

Goodrich stretched out on the poncho liner. He took his bug juice from his helmet band and soaked his face and arms. He felt the tingle of it and was almost nauseated by the airplane-glue aroma. Whew, he mused. Bugs are almost better. He took a canteen out of his low trouser pocket and drank thirstily to wash the fear out of his mouth. He couldn't quite get it all. It lingered like bile. The compound was a hulking, warted silhouette, fire-flashing, boom-emanating, an isolated, impenetrable world behind them. Theirs was a four-man other world, of zoo-kept animals turned loose in the wilderness.

All stood the first watch together, lying side by side like moonbathers. They watched the treeline through the darkling sky, studying its outer edges when the flares creaked and dropped behind it, muttering to each other about mounds and points and dips.

Finally Speedy leaned across the streambed. It was nine o'clock.

"We give Smitty first watch. I take second. Burgie third, Senator fourth." Goodrich nodded, thankful: three straight hours to sleep. Number One.

Helmet off, beside him in the grass, he slept a fitful doze, face pushed against the poncho liner. Mortar flares creaked and whistled eerily over his head. Persistent mosquitoes orbited his ears, whining. Artillery and mortar missions left the distant compound with intermittent booms. Occasionally, he woke from the haunting silence of the dead village just beyond the trees. He smelled the ash that once was hootches and was chased by haunting visions through the reaches of his dozings: it was night and the villagers, mamasans and babysans and waterbulls and dogs, crept through the sawgrass toward the streambed, teeth bared, bent on revenge. But when he would awaken there was only silent blackness. Dead ash filled the air.

Finally, thankfully, he slept.

" . . . I don't *know* what it is, Flaky. Put the Actual on. Hurry up, man." Speedy's dark eyes were fixed on the treeline. Goodrich rolled and immediately noticed the tautness that had strained the neck veins, squinched the eyes of the unflappable Speedy. He checked his watch. Eleven-fifteen.

"Roger, this is Three Charlie. We got noises out here." Pause. Speedy's eyes had not moved. "Sounds like somebody digging in. Right at the edge of the treeline. That's *most* affirm. No. I can't see shit. I don't *know* what it is."

Goodrich listened carefully, terrified. There were muffled whispers in the trees, clangs of metal in the brick-hard dirt. The metal worked a rhythm as the voices urged each other. Clang *clang* clang. *Clang* clang *clang*. Three entrenching tools, digging quickly just at the treeline's edge.

"About fifty, seventy-five meters. Roger. Right where we're s'posed to be. That's affirm." Pause, then a hoarse, louder whisper. "Well, listen, man. If you're gonna put a fire mission on it you better let me adjust. Negative. We are too *close* for eighty-ones. Roger. Maybe fifty meters." Another pause. "O.K. We'll just keep an eye on it."

Speedy woke Ottenburger, holding his head down on the poncho liner when he began to raise it. Burgie looked quizzically up at Speedy's face, then comprehended. Speedy then woke Smitty, on the other side of him, holding him down as well. He whispered as he put his meaty hand on Smitty's head. "Gooks. Shhh."

Burgie listened attentively to the spadings and grimaced,

deeply upset. "Ohhh. They got something big out there, or they wouldn't be digging it in." He nudged Speedy. "Did you ask for a mission?"

"No sixties on the hill. We're too close for art'y or eighty-ones."

Burgie scrunched back into the grassy streambed and peered behind them, at the compound. It was an unreachable island, floating in a sea of concertina. Marooned. "You're right. We are *fucked*, man."

Twenty minutes. Thirty. Muffled laughings from the treeline, growing bolder. The insistent rhythm of the clanging spades. The team hulked silently in the streambed, afraid to leave or even move for fear of becoming instant targets. They no longer dared even to whisper to one another.

Every fifteen minutes there was a barely audible chatter from the handset, which was now turned down to a whisper-silent volume. "Three Charlie Three Charlie Three Charlie, Three Three Three. If you are all secure key your handset twice, if not key it once."

One deliberate, angry squeeze.

Suddenly there were loud explosions across the river. The northern compound literally erupted. Recoilless rifles flashed and boomed, again and again, their explosions raising clouds of dirt inside the compound. Machine guns and small arms hammered at the Marines. The two-platoon perimeter fought back. Red and green tracers interlaced, careening into the black air, making weaving patterns in the night.

The artillery battery on the Bridge compound reacted. It turned its guns north and lobbed dozens of projectiles across the river, seeking to silence the attack. New bright flashes, hazes of dust, grouped around the northern compound.

Then a moment of anticipatory lull. Goodrich knew what was going to happen. He wished he could tell them in the Bridge compound. He wished he could dig a hole in the dirt and come back out in California. Watch out, he groaned inwardly, too afraid to cry. Oh, shit. Here it comes. Right now.

An avalanche of mortar rounds, timed from a dozen tubes to land together on the southern compound. Then just above the stranded team the deep pops of a heavy machine gun. Goodrich listened to himself whimper. He could not stifle it. It seemed to him a scream that would give them all away. But finally he realized that it was no more than a scratchy, whispering whine.

The Bridge compound's defenders were caught unaware, having begun to feel like spectators to the northern compound's furious defense. Bodies went flat inside bunkers, seeking cover from the mortar barrage. As they did, streams of sappers poured through the outer wire, sliding pipes of bangalore torpedoes to clear pathways through the concertina. For a moment, they were unnoticed, the explosions they created blending with the mortars. They broke through both sides of the J-shaped hill, just at its hook, tossing satchel charges of explosives into the nearest bunkers. Half of the bunkers on the artillery side, unmanned as their defenders had helped with the firing missions on the northern compound, were quickly taken by the NVA. The rest of the perimeter swarmed with creeping, dashing sappers.

Two bunkers were lost just down from third platoon's last position. The sappers manned the bunkers after killing the occupants with satchel charges, and provided a beachhead on the lines. A stream of shadows poured into the compound between the bunkers. The first cell of NVA that raced past the bunkers burned an entrance with a whooshing flamethrower. It ignited the corner of a nearby tent, and drew bright-red answers from a host of rifles fired from nearby bunkers. There was no second whoosh. Its trigger man and his mate lay dead beside low smoulders from the torchlit tent.

Another sapper team crept quickly to the center of the compound and encountered two almost identical bunkers. In its haste it demolished the chapel, leaving the command center bunker unscathed. After the chapel exploded, in a detonation that raised a bright flash and leveled the bunker in a smoking heap, another fierce mortar barrage shook the hill. The North Vietnamese would attempt to take out more bunkers, consolidate, then retreat through the breaks they had made in the wire.

Speedy's team cringed in the streambed, unspeaking, wincing as the gun cut loose again. Its explosions seemed so close that one could reach a hand up and lose it to a bullet. Each man knew that if he made an untoward move, revealing himself in any way, the whole team would not last five minutes. Nowhere to go. Nowhere to hide.

It's a twelve-seven, mused Goodrich. I've heard the stories. They can cut down trees. He hugged the ground closer, conscious of the mere inches of dirt that separated him from the cacophony above him. It seemed almost logical to him that he was going to die. The worst part was not knowing when. Maybe I should get it over with, he pondered. Stand up and let them shoot me. Maybe I should charge the gun and try to take it out. Snake would.

He looked at the others. Nobody moved. He needed to scratch a mosquito bite. He tried to go to sleep. . . .

The officers inside the command bunker had assumed control of all tactical nets, directing the defense of the compound from their underground haven. Kersey, washed in the bunker's fluorescent brightness, worked from a large composite map of the compound and its surroundings. He communicated to the listening posts, and to radios positioned in various bunkers along the perimeter, attempting to determine enemy gatherings and strong points through such reports. With that information, he would advise the battalion commander as to possible artillery missions and air strikes. . . .

Sickening crunches behind them, walking toward them, unstoppable, like a flash flood. Twirl*Boom* Twirl*Boom* Twirl-*Boom*. Eighty-one-millimeter mortars, walking toward the treeline. Twirl*Boom* just behind them Twirl*Boom* just in front of them Twirl*Boom* inside the trees.

Speedy grabbed the radio handset and whispered urgently. "Cease fire! Cease *fire,* goddamn it!" Pause. "The mortars. Three Charlie. *Charlie!* You're blowing us away with your mortars! We're too close!" Pause. "I don't give a *fuck* about the gun, man! Start giving a fuck about us!" Another pause. Speedy turned wryly to Ottenburger. "It's Kersey. *Cabron.* He says it's for our own good." Burgie grimaced tightly. "Lucky us.". . .

"Move!" Speedy was incredulous. "Where the fuck are we supposed to move *to?"* He listened for another moment. "Wait a minute." Pause. "Fuck the Colonel, wait a minute." He turned to the team. "Kersey says we gotta move. Says they're calling in eight-inchers from An Hoa to knock the twelve-seven out, and we're on gun-target line."

Smitty glowered in the dark. He had been in Vietnam a week. "I say stay, man. I ain't moving."

Ottenburger shook his head. "Ever seen an eight-incher land? We gotta move." He appeared drained, beaten. "We are truly fucked, man."

The gun opened up again, ragged rounds above their heads, as if to rankle them. Goodrich looked over to Speedy, trying to remain cool but visibly trembling. "Where?"

"I don't know. Two hundred meters left or right, he says. Two hundred fucking meters." Speedy lay flat, hugging his poncho liner in his misery. "Got any ideas?"

Ottenburger glanced over the narrow dip of streambed. He shuddered. "It ain't gonna work."

Speedy pondered it darkly, his wide face pushed into his poncho liner. Finally, he decided. "We'll crawl down the streambed. Stay low, find a good spot, lay chilly."

He grabbed the handset and keyed it. "This is Three Charlie. We're going to the left, down the streambed." Pause. "I don't know where it goes." He eyed Burgie ironically. "Probly to the gook CP." Pause. "Well, give us fifteen minutes. We're gonna be crawling."

Speedy tucked the handset into his helmet band and turned to Goodrich. "Get going, Senator. Stay low."

Goodrich did not want to leave. He began to fold his poncho liner. Maybe it'll be over by the time I fold it, he mused, comfortable with his irrationality.

Speedy crawled up and pushed him. "C'mon, stupid. Get going."

Smitty was still defiant. "Screw it. I still say stay, man."

Speedy was becoming excited. "Cool it, boot! We gotta go!"

The gun opened up again. Smitty lay flat. "I'm staying."

"Good-bye." Speedy nodded urgently to Goodrich. "Get going."

Goodrich began to crawl, staying very low, pushing the grass flat with one hand and dragging his rifle with the other. Every five or ten feet he stopped, listening to the front. Behind him Smitty rushed to catch up with the team. "Goddamn it, wait up!"

The gun opened up again, blasting the perimeter. Goodrich listened. It sounded far away, no longer threatening. He sensed that the team had at last evaded it, and came to his hands and knees, crawling faster. He wanted to reach the new position and stop moving.

Pop. An illumination flare burst above the team. Pop. Another. Pop. Another. Speedy called angrily in a hoarse whisper, "Get down, man! Freeze!"

They all lay flat. The flares burned brightly, swinging lazily on their parachutes, day-brightening the field. Speedy talked excitedly into the handset. "Tell 'em to cut the illum, man! We're sitting ducks out here! *Charlie!* Three Charlie!" Finally the last flare went dead. Goodrich lay flat for another moment, listening for movement. Speedy urged him again. "Get moving, Senator! Hurry up!" Goodrich moved to his knees and crawled quickly down the streambed.

On the point bunker of the compound a man sat beside a

large, ominous weapon, staring determinedly into an L-shaped
site, carefully cranking two wheels. He caught the movement,
saw the shadows when the flare popped. He sighted in under the
illumination, then waited for it to burn out so the backs would
raise above the ditch again. His assistant gunner had been shot by
the twelve-seven two hours before. Now comes payback, he
thought grimly.

"Fire the one-oh-six!" There was a terrific boom, a white-
hot flash of back blast. He grinned meanly. Take that, you gook
motherfuckers.

And then a figure running along the ditch that connected the
bunkers, hands in the air, screaming to the gunner: "Don't fire!
Oh, no no no! Didn't you get the word? That's the LP!"

White flash distant, heavy rush just after him, like a mini-
second of violent hailstorm. Then an angry, rolling *boom*. Gunner
was one inch of handcrank off. The fleshette round erupted just up
the hill, its centerpoint in back of Smitty. Nine thousand dart-
shaped nails saturated that portion of the field, filled the ditch,
and drove Smitty and Speedy lifeless against the streambank.

Goodrich turned when the boom rolled down and gasped.
They were both caught in the middle of a crawl, reaching down
the streambed for the haven from the eight-inchers. He stared,
feeling isolated and abandoned, and then remarked absently to
himself, through stark terror, about the surrealism of it. They
aren't even bloodied, he noted. It's as if a referee stepped in and
blew a whistle, removing them from a game. Tweeeet. You're
dead. You, too. You moved when a flare was up and you got it.
Now in a *real* war. . .

But they were really dead. The darts had saturated them so
quickly that they did not bleed, as if they both died in the middle
of a heartbeat that never finished, never pushed the blood out of
the myriad of holes.

Goodrich was in a frozen panic. That was our own gun.
They're all trying to kill us. They want us dead. Everybody wants
us dead. Speedy hated me and now he's dead. I'm not going to
make it but Speedy's dead.

"Senator." Ottenburger spoke calmly, almost sleepily. "Hey, Senator. Give me a hand, huh?"

Burgie. Oh, God. How could I forget about Burgie?

Ottenburger lay, half-hidden by sawgrass, only three feet behind Goodrich. Goodrich turned slowly in the streambed, careful not to raise his body off the ground, and crawled the inches to Burgie's face. Burgie smiled winsomely under the thin moustache, his eyes pleading with Goodrich.

Say it isn't so, Senator.

"I can't feel either leg." Ottenburger continued to smile, the eyes begging Goodrich to perform some miracle. "It's all cold, man. Everything's just cold."

Goodrich stared back uncertainly, wishing for some word that would make the past two minutes go away. Burgie's arms and face were unscratched. Maybe, thought Goodrich . . . He parted the sawgrass where the blast had spun Burgie's lower parts. The grass was wet. Burgie was a dripping ooze from the middle of his waist to his ankles.

Goodrich inhaled the heavy rich blood odor, felt his fingers slide along the oil-slick fabric over Burgie's legs, and gagged. He caught himself, and lifted Burgie's shirt to try to examine the middle parts. Then he could not hold back. He vomited into the grass, inches from Ottenburger's blood pool.

Burgie eyed him, still smiling, still hoping. "Pretty bad, huh, Senator?"

Goodrich kept his head in the grass. He retched again. I can't look at him, he thought to himself. There's nothing I can do. Can't tie him off. Can't patch him up. Can't get him out of here. Behind him, the gun opened up on the compound again.

Maybe I can call.

He inched down to Speedy's carcass and took the handset from under him. The radio was dead. He had known it would be. At least I won't have to look at Burgie if I play with it, he reasoned. He turned the knobs, banged it gently and absently keyed the handset, still petrified of the gun team in the treeline. No effect. The radio was shot to hell.

There were a lot of soldiers in the treeline. He could hear them whispering and he thought he could smell them. He thought they were laughing, celebrating, but he didn't know Vietnamese so it was just silly gook talk, up and down the music scale. He thought they stank but it could have been a waterbull pen in the ville. He thought he was bleeding all over, dripping off his crotch and chest, but it could have been sweat, or Burgie's blood, or his own vomit. His eyes burned and his arms hurt where they had scraped against the coarse sawgrass blades. He thought his arms bled, too, from the grassblades. But it could have been sweat. Or Burgie.

"Senator." The same soft, pleading voice. "Hey. Help me, man. Help me, Senator."

Goodrich turned and crawled back toward Ottenburger, pulling cautiously on the grass and pushing with his toes. Ottenburger eyed him sleepily, then burped up a stream of blood. Oh, my God, thought Goodrich. His stomach, too.

"It's all cold, Senator. Can you patch me up?" Burgie still grinned, sleepily.

The first eight-incher hit the treeline, with a terrifying, huge explosion that rent the earth, sending tree roots and huge clods dancing in the air. Goodrich and Ottenburger were covered with a veil of fresh-erupted earth.

"Help me, Senator." Then, with numb finality, "I'm gonna die, aren't I? You're just waiting for me to die." Burgie burped again. "Oh, God. Can't you patch me up?"

Goodrich peered into the ice-blue eyes, but could not hold them. "You're O.K., Burgie. You just need a doc, that's all." There was a moment of silence as all near firing abated. Goodrich felt certain that nearby enemy soldiers would hear them. "Now, hold it down, O.K., Burgie? No noise, man."

Burgie did not answer. He continued to stare at Goodrich through calm, heavy-lidded eyes. Goodrich was becoming unnerved, feeling damned by the dying Burgie.

"Patch me up, O.K., Senator? Help me, man."

"You need a doc."

Another earth eruption, an explosion so loud and close that it seemed to come from inside, to be a living part. Burgie still stared, oblivious to the dirt shower. His voice took on a fading, pleading tone, yet he still smiled hopefully.

"Can't you stop it?"

I'm in hell, thought Goodrich, over and over. I'm in hell. He crawled to Burgie's face because he was too afraid to whisper from three feet away. His own face was contorted in its fear and anguish. "*I can't.*"

"I'm gonna die. Oh, Buddhist Priest. I'm only nineteen. It's cold, Senator."

"You'll be all right."

"Don't leave me, Senator. Oh, God. Don't leave me, man."

"I won't, Burgie. I won't leave you. Now, hold it down. O.K.?"

First light. The rubble of the chapel smoked lazily, little curls of gray still reaching from the heap of blackened sandbags. There was an occasional, isolated burst of rifle fire as the last of the sappers were rooted out of bunkers and tents. The mess-hall Gunny opened up his supply tent and found an NVA soldier nonchalantly chewing on a loaf of bread, like a stuporous rat. The Gunny cut him down, sending bullets through the rations. The soldier lay dead in a pool of sugared water from canned fruit.

Along the perimeter's edge, the wire held dozens of charred treasures, blown to bits, scorched, decapitated. A mechanical mule drove along the dirt road, loading bodies to be buried later in a mass entombment outside the compound.

The concertina gate creaked open. A column of hulking, exhausted figures filed slowly down the narrow road. In front of them, the river shimmered red with sunrise. The patrol followed the outer wire and passed the inside hook of the J-shaped hill where one string of sappers had broken into the compound. There were more than a dozen bodies caught along the wire, like fish snagged randomly by a wide net.

A transistor radio cut into the silence. "Gooooo-o-o-o-ood morning, Vietnam!"

Hodges bristled. "Tell Bagger knock off the sounds."

The order passed quickly up the column. The radio went silent. The only noise now was the blunt scraping of sawgrass on their legs.

Finally Wild Man stopped. He was standing in a short ditch, among four poncho liners half-buried under clumps of dirt and branches. Hodges waved him on. "Left. Down the streambed."

Hodges peered into the looming treeline. The twelve-seven lay awkwardly on its side, half-buried under riven earth, one leg of the tripod jutting into the air. He felt his lips go tight. Well. They certainly got their twelve-seven.

Just beyond the poncho liners Smitty's helmet lay in the ditch, abandoned in his frantic crawl to catch the rest of the team. They followed the streambed for seventy meters more. Finally, the team sprawled before them, surrounded by the buzz of feasting flies and the cooked aroma of drying blood.

Wild Man halted by Smitty's corpse. The rest of the patrol bunched up behind him. They stared silently for a long moment, absorbing the gut-wrenching impact. Finally Waterbull spoke in a barely audible tone, as if he were mimicking a sportscaster.

"Senator's O.K. Senator made it."

Goodrich still sat next to Ottenburger, who lay dead over a large scab of blood that buzzed with flies. Goodrich's helmet was in the streambed and his head was between his knees, the forehead resting on one crossed arm. He looked up slowly when Waterbull spoke, then gazed numbly at the cluster that was peering mutely at him.

"I can't talk. Please. Don't ask me about it."

Hodges called to the compound for an amphtrac. Snake approached Goodrich and put an arm on his shoulder, offering him a cigarette. Goodrich pushed Snake's arm away.

"Leave me alone."

Goodrich stood with effort, and found that he was shaking

uncontrollably. He reached down to pick up his weapon and stared numbly at Burgie's corpse. His lower intestines rumbled fiercely and he felt his anus spasm wildly and he dropped his weapon, running ten feet down the streambed as he yanked his trousers open. He squatted shakily in the sawgrass and excreted a gush of brown water that was odorous with his last night's fear. He held his head in his hands, not wanting to view the rest of the squad that stood nearby. Sawgrass scratched his ass cheeks. Flies discovered his excretum and buzzed lazily below him. The sun cooked up his moisture and he was surrounded with the stench of fear. He rolled forward to his knees and retched, great dry heaves that drained a spittle of bile from his already empty stomach.

Snake walked over and offered him a canteen of water. "Take a drink, Senator. You'll feel better."

Goodrich drank with effort, still shaking. "God, I'm so fucked up."

"Put it outa your mind, man—"

Goodrich began to cry. He shuddered, his chest heaving. "Put it out of my mind? Oh, shit. What do you know? You want to see me cry? There. See? Are you happy?" Snake reached for him and he backed away, still sobbing. *"Go away."*

"You need to get some chow inside you and catch some Zs."

"I'll go myself. I don't need you. Leave me alone."

Goodrich walked back toward the compound, sobbing, catching his breath. He retrieved his poncho liner from the abandoned LP site, getting his first look at the huge gun that had caused his terror. He saw limbs and uniform pieces scattered among the clods. It upset him more.

He couldn't think. His mind was scarred from fear, bludgeoned by a new self-hate. He cried and the red dust of the road stuck to his face. His sweat melted crusts of Ottenburger's blood on the back of his hands, making rivulets of pink run down his fingers. He threw his rifle into the weeds next to the road and walked several steps, then went mechanically back and retrieved it. Neither act required a decision.

The compound was in front of him. They were still throwing

bodies onto trucks and hauling them away. The mortar crew was already firing new missions into the Arizona. Last night it had been an unreachable haven, but now it was a wire-encircled prison.

I'm in hell, Goodrich sobbed over and over. I'm in hell I'm in hell I'm in hell.

At the end of the book Goodrich, after losing most of his left leg, returns to Harvard.

THE BUILDINGS WERE THE SAME. TREES STILL sprawled thick and old. The students were only mildly different: hair a bit longer, clothing more casual, the ardent issues war and ecology rather than civil rights and Red China. But in the core they were the same: idealistic, inexperienced, waiting to be molded by some event, to react gallantly to cleanse the social order of its dark spots.

It was all the same, and yet he could no longer identify with it. He had grown beyond it, or perhaps merely away from it. His intimate rubbings in the dirt and bake of Vietnam, his exposure to minds unfogged by academic posturings, his months of near-total dependence on the strengths and skills of persons who would have been no more than laughable pariahs, or a moment of chic elbow-rub, to the students who now surrounded him, joined to make him question all his earlier premises.

It took the school experience to make him realize how much he had changed. He became something of an instant curiosity on campus, a Real Live Wounded Vet, as rare at Harvard as a miner at a tea party. He remained silent in his classes, and was alternately cynical and sardonic when called on to recite. Between classes he was recognizable on the long stone walks, a solitary, limping figure whose head was often down, who worked his artificial leg with effort and seldom looked or spoke to the ones he passed.

He would play a game with himself, walking through the hallways and the crowded cafeterias. Conversations would drift toward him from the groups of people nearby—all the subtleties and nuances of Vietnam: Moral Obligation Dominoes Containment Nuremberg Geneva Intervention Hearts and Minds ...

And he would wonder if any of them saw him limp. He tried to walk correctly, exerted much effort in his attempts. But it doesn't matter, he would muse sarcastically. I'm invisible. I'm on the ground. They can't see me, I'm too fucking *real*.

But it cut him deeply. He would often return to his small apartment rather than attend class, and sit in the dark for hours, under the wail of acid rock that belched from his stereo. He would pop a full quota of pills (the body no longer needing them but the mind craving them desperately) and once again, for the millionth time, explore the reaches of his nerve ends, searching out emotions that might help him face the empty words, and the stares that followed his limp. The stares were the worst part. And their insinuations....

He drove to the wide, flat field, scene of so many innocent events in years gone by, pep rallies and rock concerts. There was a good crowd on it, scattered here, close together there, some sitting on its outskirts in little groups as if it were indeed a picnic. There was an air of merriment among the gathered students. They were camouflaged in jeans and khaki, masked with unkemptness, almost as if they were secretly ashamed of the largeness of their own futures, or felt constrained to deny the certainties of their own lives.

Kerrigan and Braverman had arranged for him to park near the speaker's platform, along the road. He stopped the car and undid his artificial leg, as they had asked, leaving it in the car. Then he made his way up the platform, on his crutches.

The crowd had begun to chant. "HO. HO. HO CHI MINH. THE N.L.F. IS GONNA WIN."

He stood uneasily on the platform, agonizingly self-conscious of his legless state. Just below him a girl in cut-off jeans sat

comfortably on someone's shoulders. Her arms were outstretched, fists clenched, moving up and down in rhythm to the
chants. Her face smiled excitedly. Her shirt was tied in a knot
above the belly button, and unbuttoned except for the bottom two
buttons. Her breasts were huge. They also bounced with the
rhythm. Goodrich watched the breasts bounce merrily and tried to
remember if he had ever experienced such lovelies. He hadn't.

Across the field the flag came down. A new one rose. It was
red and blue, with a bright gold star in its center. Goodrich's
insides churned mightily. He told himself that he was able to
intellectualize such frivolity, that although it would have enraged
those like Snake and Bagger, he himself understood it. But soon
he stopped pretending: He was shaking with a deep rage. If he
had been stronger, he would have crossed the field and lowered
the flag himself. Or so he consoled himself as he peered at
waiting eyes, isolated on the stage.

"HO! HO! HO CHI MINH!"

And a thousand corpses rotted in Arizona.

"THE N.L.F. IS GONNA WIN!"

And a hundred ghosts increased his haunted agony.

Snake, Baby Cakes, and Hodges, all the others peered down
from uneasy, wasted rest and called upon the Senator to Set The
Bastards Straight. And those others, Bagger, Cannonball, and Cat
Man, now wronged by a culture gap that overrode any hint of
generational divide. Goodrich took the microphone and cleared
his throat. Well, here goes. He thought of them again, wishing
some of them were in the crowd.

"IT'S TIME THE KILLING ENDED." He was surprised at
the echoes of his voice that careened across the field. The crowd
cheered. It shocked and emboldened him at the same time.
Kerrigan and Braverman were watching him closely. He nodded
to them and they nodded back. Braverman was squinting. "I'D
LIKE TO SEE THE WAR END. SOON." More cheers. He gave
the two men a small smile. There. I said it. Dues are paid.

He eyed the crowd. His blood was rushing. His head
pounded from the rapid pulsing of the blood through his temples.

"ISN'T THAT WHY YOU CAME HERE? TO TRY AND END IT?" More cheers. Yeah. Groovy. End the war. "THEN WHY ARE YOU PLAYING THESE GODDAMN *GAMES?* LOOK AT YOURSELVES, AND THE FLAG. JESUS CHRIST. HO CHI MINH IS GONNA WIN. HOW MANY OF YOU ARE GOING TO GET HURT IN VIETNAM? I DIDN'T SEE ANY OF YOU IN VIETNAM. I SAW DUDES, MAN. DUDES. AND TRUCK DRIVERS AND COAL MINERS AND FARMERS. I DIDN'T SEE YOU. WHERE WERE YOU? FLUNKING YOUR DRAFT PHYSICALS? WHAT DO YOU CARE IF IT ENDS? YOU WON'T GET HURT."

He stood dumbly, staring at querulous, irritated faces, trying to think of something else to say. Something patriotic, he mused feebly, trying to remember the things he had contemplated while driving to the rally. Or maybe piss them off some more. Another putdown, like some day they'll pay. Pay what? It doesn't cost them. Never will cost them. Like some goddamn party.

He gripped the mike, staring at them. "LOOK. WHAT DO ANY OF YOU EVEN KNOW ABOUT IT, FOR CHRIST SAKE? HO CHI FUCKING MINH. AND WHAT THE HELL HAS IT COST—"

Kerrigan stripped the mike from his nerve-damaged hand without effort, then peered calmly through the center of his face, not even bothering to look him in the eye. "You fucking asshole. Get out of here."

Goodrich worked his way down the platform, engulfed by confused and hostile stares. Many in the crowd were hissing at him. He chuckled to himself. Snake would have loved it, would have grooved on the whole thing. Senator, he would have said, you finally grew some balls.

He noticed the car then. There were swastikas painted in bright red on both doors. On the hood, someone had written "FASCIST PIG." Across the narrow street a group of perhaps twenty people watched him, all grinning conspiratorially. Braverman stood at their head, holding a can of spray paint.

The paint was still wet. Goodrich smeared it around with his hand, then took his shirt off and rubbed it. The markings would not come off. Finally he stopped his futile effort and stared at the leering Braverman. He thought of flying into a rage, of jumping into his car and running over all of them, but he found that he was incapable of great emotion. It would never make any sense, and there was no use in fighting that. He swung his head from side to side, surprising everyone, including himself, by making a series of sounds that resembled a deep guffaw. Finally he raised his head.

"Fascist, huh? Hey, Braverman." He pointed a crutch. "Pow."

Then he drove away.

CHAPTER SEVEN

In October 1978, President Carter directed the Veterans Administration to conduct a survey of public attitudes toward Vietnam veterans. The study was carried out for the VA by the polling firm of Louis Harris and Associates. Issued in the summer of 1980, it included survey data comparing the views of veterans and the general public on the conduct of the war and its effects on American society.

Attitudes Toward the War

Louis Harris and Associates

A PARTICULARLY SIGNIFICANT ASPECT OF PUBLIC and Vietnam-era veterans' attitudes toward the war in Vietnam is revealed by their reaction to two projective statements included in this study:

> "The trouble in Vietnam was that our troops were asked to fight in a war we could never win."

> "The trouble in Vietnam was that our troops were asked to fight in a war which our political leaders in Washington would not let them win."

While only 38 percent of the public strongly agree with the first statement (a proportion identical to that found in our 1971 survey of public attitudes toward Vietnam-era veterans), fully 47 percent agree strongly with the second. Vietnam-era veterans are even more firmly convinced that American troops lost this war not because of a failure of arms, but rather because of a failure of the country's leadership to exercise the necessary political will. Thus, while only 37 percent of all Vietnam-era veterans strongly agree that "the trouble in Vietnam was that our troops were asked to fight in a war we could never win," fully 72 percent strongly agree that "the trouble in Vietnam was that our troops were asked to fight in a war which our political leaders in Washington would not let them win." And, while 37 percent of veterans who saw heavy combat in Vietnam agree strongly that we could never have won the war in Vietnam, fully 82 percent agree strongly that the war was lost because the nation's political leadership would not let these troops win that conflict. Among the public as a whole, those with prior military experience are those most persuaded (64 percent) that America's failure in Vietnam was a failure of the will of the country's political leadership.

The disillusionment of Vietnam veterans with the country's political leaders is further elaborated by their responses to two parallel statements. Only 37 percent of Vietnam veterans agree that "senior military commanders in Vietnam deliberately misled our political leaders in Washington about the way the war in Vietnam was going." By contrast, 76 percent of Vietnam veterans agree that "our political leaders in Washington deliberately misled the American people about the way the war in Vietnam was going."

Public and Vietnam-Era Veterans' Perceptions of the Vietnam War:
Could We Win? Were We Allowed to Win?

Q.: Let me read you some statements people have made about Vietnam-era veterans returning to civilian life. For each, would you tell me if you agree strongly, agree somewhat, disagree somewhat, or disagree strongly.

	Total Public	**Vietnam-Era Veterans**

The trouble in Vietnam was that our troops were asked to fight in a war we could never win.

(Number of Respondents)	(2,604)	(2,463)
Agree Strongly	38%	37%

	Total Public	Vietnam-Era Veterans
Agree Somewhat	27	22
Disagree Somewhat	15	17
Disagree Strongly	13	23
Not Sure	7	1
No Answer/ Refused	1	1

The trouble in Vietnam was that our troops were asked to fight in a war which our political leaders in Washington would not let them win.

	Total Public	Vietnam-Era Veterans
(Number of Respondents)	(2,604)	(2,464)
Agree Strongly	47%	72%
Agree Somewhat	26	17
Disagree Somewhat	11	6
Disagree Strongly	5	2
Not Sure	10	2
No Answer/ Refused	1	—

The assessment of both the public and Vietnam-era veterans themselves is that the impact of the war in Vietnam on the United States and American society has been overwhelmingly negative.

In the advance telephone survey of 1,200 adult Americans conducted for the Veterans Administration by Louis Harris and Associates in September 1979, we find that when asked, "What would you say have been the two or three most important effects of the war in Vietnam on the United States and American society?" most Americans find little reason to remember American involvement in the Vietnam conflict with pride. Two main themes appear in the public's responses:

> 34 percent mention the deterioration of the nation's confidence in its institutions, especially the government;
> 33 percent cite the harm done to the veterans who served in Vietnam, especially the fatalities.

Other responses volunteered by the public are also overwhelmingly negative. These include 22 percent of the public who mention negative international effects (in terms of either national prestige or refugee problems), 18 percent who cite the harm done to the economy (either through inflation or the misallocation of resources), 14 percent who say the war caused social divisiveness (between factions, generations or races) and 7 percent who cite increased drug use. The only positive effect mentioned by a substantial number (14 percent) is that the peace movement and the popular opposition to the war might help keep the nation out of other conflicted, halfhearted involvements in the future. In addition, a scant 2 percent say that the war stimulated the economy. Overall, the public's verdict is that the war was not merely a mistake, but a costly one.

The most striking of the public's volunteered statements about the effects of the war in Vietnam focus on the price paid by the veterans of that war. It has often been noted that the war in Vietnam occasioned a loss of public confidence in the country's major institutions, and it is not surprising to have this confirmed by the public in this study. Less often noted is the public's concern for the effects of the war on the veteran. The data indicate that these two effects of the war are of equal salience to the general public. There is a high level of concern among the public for the personal price paid by the veteran, in terms of both direct effects (death and disability) and indirect effects (being badly treated by the rest of society and having employment, psychological and family problems).

The members of the Vietnam Generation (those 25–34 years of age) cite most effects more often than do other age groups, reflecting the impact the war in Vietnam had on them. They place special emphasis on the effects on veterans (42 percent) and loss of public confidence in institutions (40 percent).

There is a difference in focus between racial groups. Blacks are much more likely than whites to cite the problems the war caused for veterans (blacks, 44 percent; whites, 32 percent) and much less likely to mention the loss of public confidence in institutions (blacks, 14 percent; whites, 37 percent). Blacks appear to be much more concerned with the actual problems faced by veterans and their families (especially in terms of loss of lives and problems with employment) than they are with the more abstract issue of public confidence. Women also express more concern with the problems faced by veterans (37 percent cite this) than with public confidence in institutions (28 percent). This pattern is the opposite of that shown by men, 29 percent of whom cite veterans' problems, compared to 40 percent mentioning effects on public confidence.

On the basis of the findings from the advance survey, the Harris firm further explored attitudes toward the impacts of the war.

Here, our strategy was to present the public, veterans of the Vietnam era, educators and employers with a list of problems volunteered by the public in the advance survey, and, for each, to inquire among all four groups as to whether they felt that the Vietnam War caused the problem, contributed heavily to the problem, contributed only slightly to it, or had, in their opinion, nothing at all to do with the problem.

Not surprisingly, the problem that all four groups most directly attribute to the war is the plight of the Vietnamese refugees who have become known as the "boat people."

Aside from these predictable findings, the problem that the public believes to be most related to the impact of the war on the United States is "young people's hostility toward the government," cited by 57 percent of the public as being caused, or heavily contributed to, by that war. Vietnam-era veterans (63 percent) are even more persuaded of this than is the public as a whole.

Better than half of the public and 70 percent of the Vietnam-era veterans cite the "loss of U.S. prestige and influence in other countries" as a major effect of the Vietnam war on America. An even 50 percent of the public and 60 percent of the Vietnam veterans cite "people's lack of trust in government to do what's right" as one of the war's consequences.

Other problems for which these groups see the war in Vietnam as a major causative factor include "drug abuse" and "people's lack of confidence in the country's future."

By way of contrast, less than a third of any of these four groups believe that the problems the country currently faces with respect to "alcohol abuse," "the current high rate of inflation," "the generation gap" and "problems between blacks and whites" are primarily a result of the impact the war in Vietnam has had on the United States.

In general, better-educated citizens are more likely to see these problems as being caused or contributed to heavily by the war than are the less well educated. The clear exceptions to this general pattern are with problems related to substance (alcohol and drug) abuse. Here, the less educated are more likely than the well educated to ascribe the cause of these major social problems to the impact of the war in Vietnam.

Among the public, more blacks (33 percent) than whites (24 percent) see the war as responsible for the current high rate of inflation, and blacks (38 percent) are less likely than whites (54 percent) to see the war as a major causative factor in young people's hostility toward the government or in the loss of U.S. prestige and influence in other countries.

Turning again to our cross-section of Vietnam-era veterans we note that age is often strongly related to differences in opinion about the extent to which these problems were caused or heavily contributed to by the war in Vietnam. For example, while 61 percent of the Vietnam-era veterans now 18–44 years old say that "people's lack of trust in the government to do what's right" was caused or heavily contributed to by American involvement in the Vietnam war, that proportion drops sharply among the oldest

Problems Confronting American Society Caused or Contributed to Heavily by the Vietnam War

(Number of respondents)	Total Public (2,563)	Total Vietnam-Era Veterans (2,464)	Total Educators (510)	Total Employers (1,000)
	%	%	%	%
Vietnamese refugee problem (the "Boat People")	68	74	78	72
Young people's hostility toward the government	57	63	55	54
Loss of U.S. prestige and influence in other countries	52	70	63	62
People's lack of trust in government to do what's right	50	60	51	44
Drug abuse	48	53	41	41
People's lack of confidence in the country's future	45	57	55	44
Alcohol abuse	28	33	18	17
Current high rate of inflation	26	32	31	22

Generation gap	21	26	25	20
Problems between blacks and whites	5	6	4	2

Vietnam-era veterans, those 45 or older, with a lesser 50 percent believing this to be the case.

The extent to which Vietnam-era veterans see these problems as being caused or contributed heavily to by the war is strongly associated with the degree to which they are alienated from the American political and social system. For example, while 47 percent of the "low alienation" group believe the war to have been a major causative factor in "young people's hostility toward the government," among "high alienation" Vietnam-era veterans that proportion is fully 68 percent.

White veterans of the Vietnam era are more likely to blame the war for the perceived "loss of U.S. prestige and influence in other countries" than are black Vietnam-era veterans (72 percent to 61 percent), but these black veterans are more likely than whites to see the war as the major cause of the country's current problems with drug abuse (65 percent to 52 percent), alcohol abuse (40 percent to 32 percent), and the current high rate of inflation (44 percent to 30 percent).

Expectedly, Vietnam-era veterans who believe our involvement in that conflict was a mistake or who actively resisted or demonstrated against the war are more likely than other Vietnam-era veterans to see the war as a major cause of all of these problems.

The American public takes a very positive view of the Vietnam-era veteran, and especially of those veterans who served in Vietnam itself. This is further confirmation of the public's separation of the Vietnam war from the soldiers who fought in it.

The public feels the war was a mistake but does not hold these warriors responsible for either the war or its consequences.

The public rates its feelings toward Vietnam-era veterans as very warm and overwhelmingly believes that these veterans deserve respect for their service. The public's feelings toward the veterans who actually served in Vietnam are especially warm and on a par with their feelings toward veterans of World War II and Korea. In general, the public does not see the veterans who served in the armed forces during the Vietnam era as very different from their civilian peers. The public sees these groups as more similar than dissimilar on a series of character traits.

However, the Vietnam-era veterans do not totally reciprocate the public's warmth. Their feelings toward other members of the Vietnam Generation are less warm than the feelings the public as a whole has toward this group. Vietnam-era veterans' attitudes toward their peers who demonstrated against the war or who left the country to avoid the draft are particularly cool. Vietnam-era veterans also feel that they were taken advantage of in being asked to fight "the wrong war in the wrong place at the wrong time," and that while they were away, others got ahead of them in civilian life. This feeling of being misused is especially strong among younger veterans.

Fully 83 percent of the American people strongly agree today that "veterans who served during the time the war in Vietnam was going on deserve respect for having served their country in the armed forces." This compares to a similarly high 80 percent who felt this way in 1971. Indeed, as a further indication of the high level of respect for veterans of the Vietnam era, we note that today only 15 percent of the public agree that "the real heroes of the Vietnam War are those who refused induction and faced the consequences, and not those who served in the armed forces." In 1971 that figure was an equally low 11 percent.

Thus, despite the increased feeling that "veterans who served in Vietnam are part of a war that went bad" (54 percent strongly agree today versus 37 percent in 1971), the public does not equate their participation in that ill-fated effort with personal complicity. Rather, what we detect is a growing feeling of sympathy for veterans of the Vietnam War. Thus, since 1971, the proportion of the public agreeing that "veterans of the Vietnam War were made suckers, having to risk their lives in the wrong war in the wrong place at the wrong time" has increased from 49 percent to fully 64 percent.

Comparison of Public and Vietnam-Era Veterans' Perceptions of Vietnam-Era Veterans and the War

Q.: Let me read you some statements that people have made about Vietnam-era veterans returning to civilian life. For each, would you tell me if you agree strongly, agree somewhat, disagree somewhat, or disagree strongly.

	Total Public	Vietnam-Era Veterans

Veterans who served during the time the Vietnam War was going on deserve respect for having served their country in the armed forces.

(Number of Respondents)	(2,563)	(2,464)
Agree Strongly	83%	83%
Agree Somewhat	14	14
Disagree Somewhat	2	1
Disagree Strongly	*	*
Not Sure	*	*
No Answer/Refused	*	*

---

*Less than 0.5%.

	Total Public	Vietnam-Era Veterans

The real heroes of the Vietnam War are those who refused induction and faced the consequences, and not those who served in the armed forces.

(Number of Respondents)	(2,563)	(2,464)
Agree Strongly	4%	4%
Agree Somewhat	11	8
Disagree Somewhat	25	19
Disagree Strongly	54	68
Not Sure	5	1
No Answer/Refused	1	1

Veterans who served in Vietnam are part of a war that went bad.

(Number of Respondents)	(2,563)	(2,464)
Agree Strongly	54%	60%
Agree Somewhat	27	26
Disagree Somewhat	8	7
Disagree Strongly	4	5
Not Sure	5	1
No Answer/Refused	1	1

Veterans of the Vietnam War were made suckers, having to risk their lives in the wrong war in the wrong place at the wrong time.

(Number of Respondents)	(2,563)	(2,464)
Agree Strongly	37%	28%
Agree Somewhat	27	29
Disagree Somewhat	16	22
Disagree Strongly	11	19
Not Sure	6	1
No Answer/Refused	1	1

	Total Public	Vietnam-Era Veterans

Those who refused induction during the war in Vietnam, as a matter of conscience, and were willing to face the consequences, deserve respect.

(Number of Respondents)	(2,563)	(2,464)
Agree Strongly	22%	20%
Agree Somewhat	32	32
Disagree Somewhat	17	17
Disagree Strongly	23	30
Not Sure	4	1
No Answer/Refused	1	1

Part Two

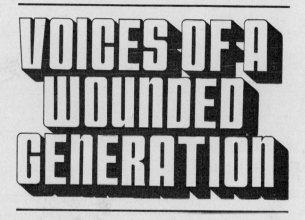

VOICES OF A WOUNDED GENERATION

CHAPTER EIGHT

A Symposium

with Philip Caputo, James Fallows, Robert Muller, Dean K. Phillips, Lucian Truscott IV, James Webb and John P. Wheeler III, with Richard Harwood, moderator

This chapter is an edited transcript of a discussion recorded in Washington in May 1980. The participants:

Philip Caputo, a Marine platoon leader who went to Vietnam with the first combat units that landed at Danang in 1965 and returned as a Chicago *Tribune* correspondent to cover the fall of Saigon in 1975. In between, he served as a *Tribune* foreign correspondent in Beirut and Moscow, winning a Pulitzer Prize. His memoir of his Vietnam tour, *A Rumor of War*, is excerpted in Part One of this book. He has also published a novel, *Horn of Africa*.

James Fallows, Harvard class of 1970, a Rhodes scholar at Oxford who became an editor of *The Washington Monthly* and *Texas Monthly*. His 1975 article for *The Washington Monthly*, "What Did You Do in the Class War, Daddy?" is excerpted in Part One. In 1976 he joined Jimmy Carter's presidential campaign as a speech writer and stayed on as chief White House speech writer until December 1978, when he became Washington editor of *The Atlantic Monthly*. His book *National Defense* was published in 1981.

Robert O. Muller, a Marine platoon leader in Vietnam in 1968–69 who was wounded while leading South Vietnamese troops in an assault. He came home permanently paralyzed from the chest down. After a year in a Veterans Administration hospital, he graduated from Hofstra Law School and became legislative director of the Eastern Chapter of the Paralyzed Veterans of America. He then founded and became executive director of Vietnam Veterans of America.

Dean K. Phillips, winner of a Silver Star and two Bronze Stars as a paratrooper with the 101st Airborne Division in Vietnam. An enlisted man, he returned with a cancer in his neck that required two major operations and chemotherapy. After a master's degree in sociology at Ohio University he moved to Colorado, received a law degree at the University of Denver and became vice chairman of the Colorado Board of Veterans Affairs. In 1977 he joined the VA's general counsel's office and in 1979 he became special assistant to Veterans Administrator Max Cleland.

Lucian K. Truscott IV, the son of a colonel and the grandson of a four-star general, is a 1969 West Point graduate who left the Army a year after graduation. He became a staff writer for *The Village Voice,* a New York weekly, and wrote *Dress Gray,* a novel about West Point.

James Webb, a 1968 Annapolis graduate, won the Navy Cross and the Silver Star as a Marine platoon and company commander in Vietnam, where he was wounded twice. After a law degree at Georgetown University, he became a counsel to the House Veterans Affairs Committee and taught poetry and the novel at the Naval Academy. He is the author of a book on U.S. military strategy and of two novels— *Fields of Fire* (excerpted in Part One) and *A Sense of Honor.*

John P. Wheeler III, a 1966 West Point graduate, was a captain with the Army's general staff in Vietnam, where he designed a logistics information system that reported the flow of men and materiel in and out of the war zone. He worked also in Washington on the staff of the secretary of defense and the Joint Chiefs of Staff. After a law degree at

Yale, he became a Washington lawyer and a cofounder of the Vietnam Veterans Memorial Fund.

The moderator was Richard Harwood, deputy managing editor of *The Washington Post,* a Marine combat veteran of Iwo Jima and other Pacific campaigns of World War II and a *Post* correspondent in the Vietnam War. He opened the session by asking each participant to introduce himself.

PHILLIPS: My name's Dean Phillips. By profession I guess you'd call me an attorney. I was in Vietnam from 1967 to '68. I volunteered to go, mainly in protest to the way the draft was going. I didn't know anything about the international aspects of whether Vietnam was right or wrong. I just didn't like the draft, which is just about the most classist, racist thing I'd ever run into headfirst. Others have written very eloquently about that. Mr. Fallows especially.

Since I returned I've spent most of my time working on issues involving veterans and lawsuits against federal agencies, things like that. Right now I'm an assistant to Cleland over at VA. The reason I moved to Washington, D.C., from Colorado was that he told me that I could deal with certain issues. One is judicial review of the VA. As you probably know, the VA is immune to court review of its benefit determinations—not only the factual questions in each individual case but also the legal questions. And its highest review body, the Board of Veterans Appeals, has to defer to VA regulations, which to me is an incredible Catch-22 situation. I was involved in changing the policy of the VA. They've always been opposed to being subjected to review.

The other issue was veterans' preference. Six years ago I assumed that the women's groups would probably attack veterans' preference in civil service hiring now that the war was winding down. Of course, veterans' preference discriminated against women as a class because so few women were veterans. It was interesting to me because they never really howled about it while the war was on. But when the war ended, I heard a big onrush of crying because they weren't veterans. So an important case was decided by the Supreme Court last June upholding us on this matter and I was involved in the government briefs on the federal level and also with the state attorney general of Massachusetts. And that's why I came to this city, to work on mainly those two issues.

WHEELER: What unit were you in?

PHILLIPS: 101st Airborne. I enlisted in the airborne in '66 and got the hell out in '68.

WHEELER: So you were a trooper?

PHILLIPS: Oh, yeah, I was with a LURP [long-range reconnaissance platoon] team for six months. I got nicked a couple times but nothing like other people sitting at this table have gotten hurt. I will say that I came out pretty strongly against the war when I returned. Very loudly and publicly. I think you were in Vietnam Veterans Against the War in '71, Bobby, and I joined it but I was in Denver trying to get through law school. I didn't come down to Washington when they raised all the hell. But now that there's discussion of resuming registration for the draft, frankly I'm in favor of that. I didn't think I'd come to that ten years later, after my feelings in '71 and '72, but I'm taking some action in my own life, in my own way, to make my commitment to the 18-to-20-year-olds. I'm trying to get into the reserves at least. I used to hate the reserves; it used to be a way to duck active duty. I'm working on that now. [At the end of 1980, he received an Army Reserve Commission as an infantry captain.]

If I've readjusted at all, it's been because of my wife. She just passed the Virginia Bar. Now she's a lawyer. I met her when she was an emergency room nurse. She took care of me pretty well, I guess. If there's any stability in my life, it's mainly because of Carla.

MULLER: My name is Bob Muller. I started an organization that is now called Vietnam Veterans of America. It started almost 2½ years ago. Its purposes are many and varied. Most simply stated, it is to try and provide the still-needed measures of assistance for the Vietnam veteran, to meet their needs that are attributable to their military service. It is to try and provide, beyond a measure of assistance for their particular needs, a measure of recognition and appreciation for what their experiences were and still are. It is to try and go beyond those two basic points to try and help America by our being the catalyst in the process of coming to terms with the experience of Vietnam.

I joined the Marines when I was a senior in college, back in May of '67. I was born in Geneva, Switzerland, with the name of Olivier Robert William Muller, Olivier for peace. It was in 1945. My parents were born and raised in a small town up in the Alps. My father worked as a precision machine tool engineer and was sent by his company to America to service precision machine tools. I came here as a young child. We grew up in a middle-income family in New York City and subsequently on Long Island. I went through junior high and high school in Great Neck, Long Island, which is an affluent, liberal community. I went to college originally to become a coach. Physical education major for a couple of years. Transferred to Hofstra University and became a business major. When I was a senior, and I was on dean's list consistently and I was very go-go in business, my professors advised me that I had better have military experience on my resumé lest people would think I was a funny duck, and I was well advised of the fraternal nature of Wall Street firms, etcetera, and it would be a leg up and, my God, if I ever had any combat, as leadership experience that was yet another couple of points. Walked on campus one day and there was this Marine in dress blues looking real sharp and I said that looks good, let's do it. And with that, went in. Became honor man in my platoon and, while I went in with basically a willingness to serve, I came out of Marine Corps training a basic lunatic. I *demanded* infantry, *demanded* Vietnam as my duty station, and I got what I wanted. I lasted for eight months, served as a platoon commander, then company commander. Then I worked with MACV—military assistance command—as an adviser to ARVN [South Vietnamese army] units for four months. Subsequently I did get shot, became a paraplegic. Came back stateside, spent a year at a VA hospital, got out, thought that law was the way to affect society, went to law school, got a law degree, worked with the paralyzed veterans, left them to start the undertaking for the Vietnam veterans.

WEBB: I'm Jim Webb. I'm now the minority counsel to the Veterans Affairs Committee, House of Representatives. I grew up in a military family with my roots in the South, principally Kentucky and Arkansas. Went to the Naval Academy. Went into the Marine Corps after that. Once I left the Marine Corps, went to law school. I write, and there are times when I would like to think of myself as an attorney, although they're not very often.

I think the most veiled issue out of Vietnam, one that Jim Fallows is one of the few people to write courageously about, is the cleavage within the generation, the polarization, almost culture by culture, within our age group. And we must be very careful how we define culture. Culture keys on geographic area, it keys on ethnic background, it keys on profession, it keys on education, but the accumulation of those things probably were a greater determinant as to how people felt about societal duty during Vietnam than any other area. And for the most part, the generation, I think, has been maligned with respect to its beliefs about societal duty. I think that this in many cases was furthered by institutions that did not understand how you deal with the war. We had an accumulation of people on college campuses during the war. They were readily available. They were grouped. They made good media and, in my opinion, they did not represent what was going on totally, fully, in our generation. They represented a valid viewpoint. They did not represent the whole pastiche.

This has been a concern of mine since I left the Marine Corps and went into Georgetown Law School. I went from an environment where Vietnam was the totality of our experience—I went over with 67 lieutenants and 22 of them were killed—to an environment where in three years, in a student body of 1,800 people, I met three people who'd been in combat in Vietnam.

And it would not leave my head and that is, in effect, why I began writing.

My greatest concern is on the effects in a society as to how it views itself, as to what values are now going to be passed down by our generation. We came out of a period where dissent became probably the most legitimate form of dealing with government. Not just through Vietnam. We fail to think in terms of the accumulation of the dissent issues when we try to pull Vietnam out. We had civil rights: 1964—the Civil Rights Act was signed; 1964—the Gulf of Tonkin resolution was signed; 1968—the war peaked; 1968—Martin Luther King was killed. They intertwine. The effect, though, was that the primary way to deal with government in our age group as it was cutting its teeth was to dissent. And what values now are being passed down, either through our progeny or through the people that we deal with in any position of responsibility in a bureaucracy? I look to military service, of course, as a societal duty. I feel very strongly about it. But I also wonder, given the confusions of that time period, which were legitimate for every individual, how a person who in the context of history committed an antisocial act, whether it was valid at the time or not, now deals with it when he has to look at his children and at the people that he deals with in any institutional sense and when they are confronted with the notion of whether they have a duty in some way to serve their society.

You can see that most clearly right now in the issue of the draft. We have right now probably the most inequitable draft imaginable. We have an economic draft. An army that by 1982 is going to be 42 percent black in its lower enlisted ranks, and that's not including the browns, the other minorities, and white enlistees with a lower educational level than the blacks. And how are people dealing with it and why? What sort of self-image questions interfere in the logic of saying that we need a draft? These are the sorts of things that bother me.

FALLOWS: I'm Jim Fallows. I now work for *The Atlantic Monthly* magazine. I've been a journalist most of my working

life, about eight years or so. I grew up in a little town in
California, in an upper-middle-class family. My father is a doctor.
My father was, I guess, 15 when World War II started and 19 when
it ended. His older brother was a foot soldier in Europe. My father
enrolled in the V-12 [Navy college program] to become a doctor
and was a Navy doctor during the Korean War. When I was
growing up I was in high school in this town, Redlands, Calif.,
from '63 to '66, and there were the only first faint ripplings of
complaint about the war then. This was a town that Goldwater
nearly carried in 1964. Everybody that you knew was a Republican or of that bent. So when I went off to college at Harvard
in the fall of '66 I had no inkling at all that there might be reason
to question this war that was going on at the time. I remember the
first thing which stuck in my mind was a speech that Arthur
Goldberg came to give at Harvard that winter, in January of '67.
He was going to debate one of the Harvard professors about the
war. So I heard the professor's case at length and I thought, well,
now there'll be the answers from Arthur Goldberg. And Arthur
Goldberg spoke for about an hour and there were no answers at
all. None of the points were rebutted. And that sticks in my mind
as the time when I began to wonder about the wisdom of the
enterprise.

By the end of the four years I was at Harvard, by 1970, the
conventional wisdom among everybody I knew and me too was
that the war was a misguided enterprise and there was at that time
a suppressed version of what has probably become a more deeply
suppressed tension now, which is: How do you reconcile your
sincere and deep opposition to a policy with your knowledge of
what the class and social effects are of exempting yourself from
what was going on? Now, the way that took place in college,
which I've written about perhaps to excess, is that almost
everybody I knew from Harvard or similar colleges found some
trick ways out of the draft, as I did myself, and everybody blinded
themselves to the long-run consequences of this, of who was
going when you weren't going yourself. There was a side of this
which is explicable as the behavior of people under pressure.

There was a side of it which was most noxious, I think, which was the idea that the war machine would be brought to a halt if it were denied our bodies and that was sort of the pep talk everybody gave themselves, that this was the way to stop the war. And of course it is patent now that exactly the opposite took place: The more the burden of the war was shifted on families who had the least influence, the longer the war went on. So that was the experience with the war that I grew up with.

Five years after the time I had gotten out of my draft I wrote an article in *The Washington Monthly* called "What Did You Do in the Class War, Daddy?" which was trying to go into some of these things. I guess I find myself in a very awkward position talking about these things, because on the one hand I feel that there is a point to be made about the cleavage within our generation that all of you have talked about. I've gotten a little tired of making that point myself for a variety of reasons, the least of which is hate mail, which is sort of a daily staple in life. I think the more serious reasons why I'm tiring of this are first, one's aversion to sounding like a scold. That is a pose that nobody wants to take and I don't want to take. Second is, there is an overtone in this of wearing the hair shirt and guilt, which is not the point that I think needs to be brought out. There is a necessary stage of everybody purging their guilt, and there are different sorts of burdens that different people bear. But the real thing that needs to be done for people of our vintage, I think, is at least to face what went on and try to reconcile the different camps of our generation, because otherwise I think there is a sometimes deeply and sometimes not so deeply suppressed resentment and grudges of one sort or another of all of these different parts of our vintage for the other parts. And unless those are examined and brought out I think we'll be in trouble in the long run. I fear a backlash if these things aren't talked about fully enough. People will become big militarists to try to prove that this part of their background is not something to be ashamed of. So that is why, while I am personally tired of talking about these things, I think it is crucial to have some venting of them among our people.

WHEELER: I was born while my father was in the Ardennes getting his tank company taken apart by the Germans during the Battle of the Bulge. I'm an Army brat and I spent 20 years growing up traveling around the world with my pop and our family. I went to West Point and graduated in '66. I got good grades so I went into artillery. I think I learned a little bit at West Point about war. I think I picked up enough to know that this war was not well guided. At any rate, I took an opportunity I had, as an academy graduate with high enough class standing, to go to Harvard. At the same time Jim Fallows was there writing on the *Crimson,* I sat at the business school getting an MBA.

I then went to the Army general staff in Long Binh in Vietnam and worked on logistics matters and I lived in the *M*A*S*H* subculture. You know that *M*A*S*H* is about Vietnam. That's where I lived. The helicopters coming in every day. The dead men and the wounded men and the crazy ladies and all the doctors. That was Long Binh. In other assignments, I worked in the office of the secretary of defense. I studied biological warfare and other matters of strategic analysis. And then I worked on the Joint Staff for a year as a hired Russian, assuming the role of a Soviet nuclear strike planner to test our defenses. I went to law school after that and decided it wasn't a soldier I wanted to be for the rest of my life. Went to Yale, graduated, clerked for a year and practiced law.

My main concern is the one that we're putting our finger on here. There's a fracture in our generation and it was struck by the Vietnam War. The demographics, I think, are that there were 30 million men in our generation, roughly, who matured, say '63 maybe to '70. If that's right, then there would be another 30 million women, roughly. And what that shows is that we're the baby boom generation. We're a large chunk of people moving through our society over time, a huge lump of young people. Out of the 30 million men, there are 3 million who served in the combat zone.

WEBB: As I understand the figures, there are 27 million and 2.7 million. Something like that.

WHEELER: The reason I bring it up is you say "the Vietnam War" and the period defined 3 million men who went into the combat zone. I think that's true and self-evident. I think that when you talk about a fracture in our generation that it would be tempting to say, "But the other 27 million men and roughly 30 million women were perhaps not so formidably affected by the war." But I just don't think that's true. And the way I phrase that question is to wonder if, to pick a name and with all respect for his courage, was Tom Hayden defined politically by the Vietnam War? I think the answer is yes. The war was a mold, and to understand our generation if we look at the mold I think we can see how the different pieces got broken.

WEBB: If we're going to talk figures, we should say that there were almost 9 million people who wore the uniform during that period and many of them who were here stateside were as affected by having to wear the uniform as someone who was in some of the areas in Vietnam.

WHEELER: Thinking about a fracture in these terms, where I've come out in terms of suspecting a result is that the men who served in the combat zone have something distinctive to offer and that there are some barriers to letting us do that. And I'd like to put my finger on what it is distinctive we have to offer, what can be done about enabling us to do that. And I suspect the mainspring of that for us would be the process we went through in getting to the war zone and a sense of allegiance to the men who are dead.

TRUSCOTT: I'm Lucian Truscott. I was born in Japan, raised in the Army. By the time I was 18 I'd lived in 30 houses or something. Went to West Point, graduated in 1969, went into the Army, got kicked out of the Army a year later for writing for *The Village Voice* and at the same time didn't go to Vietnam because, to make a long story short, I had a conversation with a lieutenant general on the telephone from my trailer in Colorado Springs, was threatened to be sent to Vietnam punitively if I didn't withdraw an article I had written for publication, and I threatened to sue him if he did anything like that. I never went and I got kicked out. And then I went to work for *The Voice* for five years, then I free-lanced for a while, then I wrote a book and now I'm writing books.

My interest is in these demographics: 27 million people coming of age during the war. And I really don't think we have to define what the war years are. Basically we're talking about ten years of Americans. And ten years of American men. And if you got 27 million who came of age and 9 million who served, that's 18 million who didn't. That's twice as many that didn't serve. Not to mention 30 million women that didn't serve. The way that I look at this thing is to look at it sexually, basically from the standpoint of the war between the sexes. Now what went on during this whole time, when there was also the civil rights movement, the women's movement came of age. But it wasn't just the women's movement, it was all kinds of things going on in the work force: 49 percent of the women between the ages of 18 and 45, I think, work now; 49 percent have jobs, full-time jobs. And if you go back ten years or you go back to 1964, the beginning of the war, I don't know the figure but I would imagine it's well below 20 percent. So all kinds of things have happened between men and women during these years and I think that the most profound difference between men and women, aside from the obvious sexual one, is that during those ten years every single guy who came of age in this country who didn't just up and go to Canada immediately had to make an extraordinarily profound moral decision about that war awfully quickly: whether or not they were going to register for the draft, go to jail, dodge the draft, continue valid or at least legal ways of getting out of the draft. We can all remember what they were: going to college, and then it was getting married, and then they did away with that one, and then it was becoming a teacher, and then they did away with that one, but basically it boiled down to, by about 1970, if you had a thousand dollars a year you could do it.

I'll give you a good example: In Connecticut, 47 percent of those who registered for the draft never even went for a draft physical, and of those who went for a physical, the final total was about 21 percent of 18-year-olds who came of age during those ten years got drafted. Now we all know that Connecticut is a very affluent state and there's a lot of people with a thousand bucks a year in the state of Connecticut.

And my interest is in what's really becoming more and more, not less and less, a deep division between men and women in this country because it really centers around the war. I can recall back in those days, having short hair and being at West Point, you were damned if you did and damned if you didn't. Every woman you ever went out with thought you were going to be completely fucked up if you did go to Vietnam, on the one hand. But then there was always an undercurrent that if you don't go to Vietnam then there's going to be something wrong with you as a man, because we all know that civilizations have constantly over the course of history called upon people to go and fight wars whenever wars have come along. And the people they've called upon have been men. And I think the fact that women were not confronted with this decision that everybody had to make that was a guy back then, and were left free during those years to pursue the kinds of careers that make 49 percent of these women now part of the work force and to increase the number of their enrollments in law schools and whatever, I think that that's an extraordinary result of this war and I think that too little attention has been paid to that as an issue in general and I think that too little attention has been paid to the 18 million guys who didn't go into uniform.

WEBB: It's not just a question of the battle between the sexes. It's a question of sexuality and just as important is: What about those 18 million men?

TRUSCOTT: That's what I came here to talk about, because if you want to do anything from now in this country you can't depend on the Vietnam War veteran vote. You know, you can't get five Vietnam veterans together to agree on which was a better unit, you know, much less who to vote for, or what kind of hat was better to wear, or anything else. And so you've got to come to grips with this extraordinary number of people who didn't go into uniform. I think a lot of guys are now in a position where they're questioning not so much whether they did their duty to their country and so forth, but whether or not they did their duty as a man. And increasingly during those years, and even more so today, I think that guys are walking around wondering how are you supposed to act as a guy. Nobody really knows how to act anymore. "Macho" became a dirty word during these years. Macho used to be an OK thing to be.

Here's a perfect example. When we were growing up, macho was when you were playing football, when they hiked the ball if you knocked over the other guy and he went down and you were still on your feet, the coach kicked you in the ass and said "Hey, baby, that was macho!" Now these guys go out and run 20 miles, which is absolute masochistic self-punishment, and they brag about it. And that's macho! They're not knocking the other guy down, they're knocking themselves down. There's a perfect example of 180-degree flop of self-image. It used to be cool to hit the other guy, and now you're supposed to hurt yourself.

WEBB: Betty Friedan had a comment that was quoted in one of the papers a couple of weeks ago that the 1980s are the period for males in our society to redefine what their role is. In the '70s the women did it and now in the '80s the men are going to do it and she said, and this is a pretty straight quote, "Machismo is dead. It died in Vietnam." And my reaction to that is no, it didn't die in Vietnam. If it died at all in this society, it died among the people who had to question who they are as a male because, through one way or another, they avoided what is the quintessentially male function in a society, and that's going into uniform. They're having to deal with that.

WHEELER: What's the "quintessentially male" thing again?

WEBB: Defending your society. Taking up arms and defending your society, in the history of the world and every civilization that exists today.

HARWOOD: You guys are all very successful and intelligent and articulate. To what extent can you speak for the mass of your fellows, the other 8 or 9 million people who put on the uniform during those years or the 20 million who didn't? If you went down to Fordyce, Arkansas, and to the gas station and there's some guy pumping it there who did his two or three years as a grunt, would he be talking this way? Would he be "fractured," traumatized or whatever?

TRUSCOTT: Well, I grew up with the Army in the '40s and the '50s. I grew up in a basically middle-class, but a lower-middle-class, society. I guess when my old man was a captain he was probably earning $175 a month or $200 a month. Nobody had any money. When you were a kid, you could see kids out playing with cap guns—all our fathers sat down and carved them out with a hacksaw. I would never pretend to speak for these people, but I certainly grew up with them and was around them. And then in the Army, being a platoon leader, those were the guys that were in my platoon. One of the biggest problems I had as a platoon leader at Fort Carson was guys who would re-up [reenlist] to buy a car. Here's a guy who was going to re-up for six years because the bonus just went up another grand. And locking themselves in and they didn't really want to be in the Army and they hated it. I traveled around the country my last two years with *The Voice* talking to a lot of people about these things. I really don't think there are any class boundaries when it comes to the kinds of suffering that's going on, the kinds of fallout that we've just been talking about here. If you go into the Army, my experience in talking with people who were in the Army and their various disillusionment, embitterment, pride or whatever, there were lieutenants from Vanderbilt University who were just as pissed off about Vietnam or just as proud as GIs from the hills of Kentucky. I could really never detect a whole lot of differences in personal opinions about the war from guys who served over there that just ran strictly along class lines. In fact, there's almost an opposite effect, to a certain extent, that those who were getting screwed the worst, the guys who couldn't get out of the war and really had the biggest reason to gripe if they were going to, gripe the least about that specifically.

WEBB: I keep up with nine or ten people out of my platoon,

people who served under me, and a number of them are very close friends of mine and I get some pretty good feedback from them. The final scene in my book is a scene where a guy goes back to Harvard. He just got his leg blown off and he says some very angry things to a crowd after having been pushed into speaking at an antiwar rally after the Cambodian incursion. And the reaction to that final scene within our age group is almost completely split. I have literally a hundred letters from people who were former grunts saying, "Dammit, somebody finally said it." At the same time I can look at reviews from people—you know, a professor of English at such and such a college—who will say, "Webb's book is really good until the final scene," because it was very obviously where they were coming from. So I think the issue really is defined and there are some objective ways to show that.

FALLOWS: I had a professor-of-English reaction to the final scene, because it did not resemble what I remember from my time at that school. But I think the reason it has touched off the kind of emotions that you talk about is that it is the explicit laying down of the glove. It is where you make the accusation, and that is opening up the suppressed wound or the partially closed wound.

WEBB: To further define the cleavage, in May 1970 I was stationed at Quantico, at OCS [officer candidate school], and when the lid went off the enlisted people who were assigned to OCS, the instructors, aggressors on the operations and this sort of thing, most of these people were recently back from a tour in Vietnam and hadn't seen their family in a year. And while colleges cancelled classes in order that people could go down on the Mall and do whatever they were doing on the Mall, large numbers of these guys were locked into rooms 25 percent the size of this room. We'd sit in there for an entire weekend, 30 guys in a room packed in with a PRC 25 radio, waiting to be called to go down to Washington or to the main gate of Quantico or whatever, and I never saw the bitterness in Vietnam that I saw in those rooms.

TRUSCOTT: The way I would describe it is the feeling was of being discriminated against. When I was at West Point, people used to come up from New York all the time because it was 50 miles away and it was the closest uniforms around. Fort Dix was Jersey—nobody wanted to go there. West Point was pretty. Vassar girls used to come over and demonstrate. Guys that were there resented the fact that they were coming down the street at West Point where all these people were being trained to go and fight in Vietnam and they never went out and demonstrated at the Harvard Business School, where they were being trained to go down and sell war stocks, war profiteering. That was the boom-boom years—there were guys who cleaned up and got out in those years selling Dow Chemical and every other damn thing. And people felt discriminated against and embittered.

"I wanted to go there and wipe that restaurant out."
—Philip Caputo

At this point Philip Caputo joined the group and was asked to introduce himself.

CAPUTO: I was born on the West Side of Chicago of Italian parents. In my case it was fourth-generation, but it was a working-class family. I came from that level of society that I would say supplied most of the enlisted men in the war, and it was just by kind of a freak that I was an officer by the time I got over there.

I was in the Marines. Like Jim, I was a platoon commander for most of the time I was over there. About three or four months, I was on a regimental staff. I had gone over there when the shooting match started in 1965. And, of course, one of the odd things about that war is it was so amorphous, it had no concrete beginning. There was no Pearl Harbor, no North Koreans going over the DMZ or anything like that. When I say it "started" it was with the first commitment of American ground combat forces, and that happened to be the brigade that I was with. And I was there a total of 16 months, which is three months over the normal

13-month tour. If you've read the book, you know why I was there for the extra three months. I was under investigation for what I kind of call a miniature My Lai, when a squad that I had sent into a village killed a couple of Vietnamese civilians whom we had thought to be Viet Cong and turned out not to be. And so there was this rather lengthy investigation that was leading up to a general court-martial for five of the eight men who were involved and myself. Six of us altogether. And a lot of people have said, "What did you do in the war?" And I've said that I was recommended for a Bronze Star for heroism and recommended for a general court-martial, and received neither.

TRUSCOTT: Seems like a fair exchange.

CAPUTO: That was the extent of my brilliant military career.

HARWOOD: I gather you were a normal red-blooded American boy when you went over, gung ho. And how did you come out?

CAPUTO: When we went over in '65, when I think back about it, I feel as if emotionally, attitudinally, we were, all of us, much closer to our fathers' generation than we were to people who were, let's say, freshmen when we were seniors. The people who were only four to five years younger than I seemed totally different in the way they looked at the world than I did, at least at the time that I went over. Now I came back extremely embittered, but that was probably due to the peculiar circumstances and what happened to me over there. Obviously, that kind of investigation, while it was perhaps more common than we care to believe, wasn't anything like a universal experience. But when I came back I was not only embittered but I think not healthy psychologically. It must have been five or six years before I began to feel mentally integrated again.

I used to get reactions of inexplicable anger, almost a fury, that would just come over me like that. When I was first going out with the girl who's now my wife, we were in a restaurant one night. I was shortly out of the Marines. I remember we were in a restaurant and I was looking at everybody, and I knew what was going on over there. I still had all sorts of buddies of mine who were over there, and in fact I had recently heard about one who had gotten killed. And I was watching everybody eating dinner and they were all well dressed and everything, and she said, "What's the matter?" And I said, "Let's get out of here. In about two minutes I'm going to get up and start busting heads." And I said, "I don't know why." I wanted to go there and wipe that restaurant out. It was so strong in me. My whole body was tensing up.

And that was followed in about an hour or two by this black depression, almost like I felt guilty about feeling so infuriated that I got very, very depressed about the whole thing. And I was undergoing those kind of side waves, emotions going like this, all the time, to the point where there was a period in my life where it seemed like the only emotion I was capable of was rage. And I think that—not to get ridiculously personal about the whole thing—that the reason I married the girl I did was because she was the only person I could be around that I didn't feel like breaking her jaw.

And for a long time I thought, well, this is me, I'm crazy, I'm a madman. But after I wrote the book, I've received probably five or six hundred letters and almost every one of those letters that's from a combat veteran, as compared to the guy who ran the pizza parlor in Saigon, said the same thing: that they had these same inexplicable, unstable emotions, of which it seemed that anger was the dominant one. And then they talked about how it became, in their own lives, a frozen rage, which I think creates a kind of depression—I've heard psychologists define depression as a kind of frozen rage—to the point where they can't even express anger any longer. And they said that at least one good thing that the book did for them is that they recognized themselves in it and it was kind of a purgation for them.

WEBB: Yeah, I went through law school the same way.

TRUSCOTT: Every guy I know—guys who went to Vietnam and even guys who didn't go to Vietnam—in the Army went through the same ups and downs and black rages. I would just note that while all this was going on and all these people were feeling rage, the women's movement had picked "rage" as their favorite word.

I remember a story by Gloria Steinem, "What Are We Going to Do With Our Rage?" You know, when are we going to get our husbands to help us with the dishes? I mean, that word was just beat to death.

CAPUTO: It's the same people that like to bandy the word "guilt" around. Guilt and rage—you could pick it off your emotional supermarket shelf and say, "Well, I'll feel this now and then I'll put it back." But I don't think any of them know what it's like to feel the kind of rage that I think might motivate some criminals into criminal acts. That kind of destructive, antisocial feeling.

PHILLIPS: I felt anger because I was with a platoon of 26 people and five of us came out in one piece. And I had the feelings you had, like I'd go into a public place where people my age, it was business as usual or it appeared to me to be business as usual. And I thought to myself, Jesus Christ, you know, one of my best friends is blown in half and I keep thinking about that and here is this fucker sitting over here and the most important thing in his life appears to me to be whether the Dodgers win the pennant. I don't really know what cross that person is bearing, but I felt an alienation.

When I was in Vietnam Veterans Against the War for six months, or whatever I was in, I didn't think that we spoke for all veterans. But I still felt that there was something to say there and it was said in a few months, at least for me, and then I got out of it. I was anti-Vietnam War, I just thought the war was wrong. Fine. But there were other groups that were pro-North Vietnam. And I said, "What the fuck's going on here? I'm not pro-fucking-North-Vietnamese." Our group was different in that way. We didn't get along. At least I didn't get along with the other groups that were against the war. But I still had to make my statement, you know. And it took months to get my shit together to say it, and maybe I still don't have it together because I feel strongly about it.

When I applied to graduate school, the admissions committee was three people. One of them was a professor who didn't want any Vietnam vets accepted at the graduate school. It's incredible. They were blaming the war on the warrior. I know it's trite and all this shit. But it's true. And I thought to myself, look, I didn't come here and say, "Hey, I'm a veteran and here's a few rows of decorations and I want some." I wanted to forget it. I wanted to melt back into society. But the thing was, they wouldn't let me. Here I am, a supposed liberal, right? Still very much pro-ERA. Yet many of the liberals, or the people who saw themselves as liberals, would label me a fucking right-winger. Look, I've got a master's degree in sociology—I practically had to sue to get it. Really. Because I was hassled, harassed....

WEBB: I do not think that there has been enough recognition by society that this sort of thing went on. In the [Allen] Bakke "reverse discrimination" case, *The Washington Post* did an interview with the one member of the board who had voted in favor of Bakke's admission, his initial application [to the University of California medical school at Davis]. And his comment was that the other two people had felt very strongly against admitting Bakke because he had been a Marine.

PHILLIPS: And he was a Vietnam vet, too, wasn't he? He was a captain in 'Nam. He was in ten months.

CAPUTO: Well, I had never run into any discrimination in my personal life after I got out nor did I know anybody that happened to, personally, but I have come across cases in the press. It still angers me, because I still think there is a residue of that feeling among people who were ideologically committed not to the inhumanity of the war but either to some kind of national self-flagellation or to seeing the "agrarian reformers" take over. My heart was never in the antiwar movement. I didn't get into it until two things had happened. I had covered the Kent State massacre. And I was on the side of the students, because I interviewed the National Guard commander and I was saying, "Why did you guys..."

PHILLIPS: Was this the major general?

CAPUTO: No, this was the guy who was on the ground, he was either a captain or a first lieutenant. And I said, "Why did you just fire into this crowd? I know they were hassling you." And he made this description that sounded like something out of a Kipling novel—the Thin Red Line, and here come the fuzzy-wuzzies, and he says, "We had no choice but to, you know, 'First rank, kneel!'" And he's giving me this stuff and going on and on and I got PO'd at him and said, "Look, asshole, I've been *really* shot at," and then he nearly threw a brick at me. And that started turning me around.

PHILLIPS: He was a guy who didn't have Vietnam combat experience.

CAPUTO: No, no.

PHILLIPS: Most of them joined the National Guard to dodge the draft.

CAPUTO: They're draft dodgers.

PHILLIPS: They called up 3 percent of the Guard and reserves during the whole fucking war. Just 3 percent. Most of those were noncombat units. I'm from Ohio, lived near Kent State. These guys saw themselves as patriots. "By God, I enlisted. I'm in the Guard or the reserves."

CAPUTO: But the big thing was that when that guy [John] Kerry got up and started making a speech. Now, whatever his personal motives were, his political ambitions, he did say a lot of things that echoed things that I felt. And so, with him and the formation of the Vietnam Veterans Against the War, I felt, well, the only people who have a *right* to say anything against the war—and I still feel that way—were the ones who were there, who had suffered through it. But again, when I was in that organization, you know, we did have contact with the other antiwar organizations and I had the same exact reaction to them. I didn't like them. And I used to get to some points where I would deliberately get outrageous. I would deliberately try to upset them. I recall that there was one meeting where there was a group from the Vietnam Veterans Against the War and another group from the SDS [Students for a Democratic Society] and another group. I walked into the place wearing a supertight Quantico Marines sweatshirt. It says "U.S. Marines, Quantico, Va." And I had that on and I kind of walked in flexing and acting like I was going to go bust somebody up. And just to upset them, put them off balance. Almost like I wanted them to hate me.

PHILLIPS: You judge somebody by his enemies as well as his friends. I felt the same way.

HARWOOD: Bobby, you didn't come back as a sprinter. What about rage?

MULLER: Rage is something that I continually work at to control. Were it not for the fact that I met the woman who is my wife, I'd be dead today, I am convinced. Because I would have taken a rifle and just made very public my sentiments. My wife literally has saved my life through finding the love that we've developed in our relationship and the ability to temper what's in me and give it a practical and effective application.

When I came back, I had been the officer, I had been normally in charge of everything that there was going in the field, because I was senior man and, in the Marine Corps especially, I was God. All right? When I said, "Go left" or "Go right," it was done, and there'd be no questions asked. Plus there's a very strong sense of power when you can call in jet strikes, artillery and the battleship New Jersey. You know: massive ego trip. Lots of power. To come into the VA hospitals and become the veteran and literally have a GS-5 who's got 20-something years perhaps in, slow-stepping guy, who balks when you ask if he would get you a pitcher of water because you can't get out of bed, and you've got to ask him three times.

It started to build, the sense of anger. When I was summarily dismissed, as I was by the doctors and by other people in the VA system, I, who had always been very dutiful and very respectful of authority, made a decision. Very quickly. That if I was to survive, I had to fight back and I had to go against the people that I was naturally inclined to be deferential to. Namely, doctors. Foremost. And I started to speak up. Literally, for reasons of survival. Borne out by the fact that eight of the guys on my spinal-cord injury wards have committed suicide since I was in the hospital. Including my closest friend. *Life* magazine came in and

did a cover story, right at the time of Kent State, on my ward and I
was there. And it was the largest-selling issue *Life* ever put out.
Cover story on the neglected wounded. I was the spokesman for
the guys. So I started doing some media, some television,
etcetera. I had guys from VVAW come by and talk to me because
of my visibility. And I gravitated toward VVAW and I became a
spokesman, although never a member. I was identified nationally,
but I couldn't surrender my very individual sense to anything,
including VVAW, as much as I could agree with a lot of it.

Every single Vietnam veteran that I knew was a member of
VVAW. I did not know a Vietnam veteran who was not in great
sympathy with what we were going through collectively, most
notably in public here in '71, with throwing the medals back.
Every one of my friends went through the antiwar process,
eventually flipping out, freaking out and going to the woods,
going away or whatever. Some for a period of years, to settle
within themselves their experiences. And basically all of them
have put it together and are doing something with their lives in
one way, shape or another. I realized, as I started with this
Vietnam veterans' organization that we got going here, that my
experience, which I thought was the predominant experience of
Vietnam veterans in this country, is clearly the minority experience. What I found was that those of us who gravitated toward
VVAW—and who did so, by the way, mainly not for the politics
of the organization, of opposing the war, as much as for the
opportunity to have a peer group, to have guys that you could
relate to. It was a forum to meet other guys, to share experiences
and to rap it through. That is what the overwhelming majority of
Vietnam veterans across the country have never had. Not only is it
my personal experience in traveling for the past couple of years
across the country, but the studies are coming back and saying
that. When [Arthur] Egendorf from the Center for Policy Research received a million-dollar contract from the Veterans
Administration to survey Vietnam veterans around the country as
to their readjustment problems, etcetera, they randomly selected

guys and they found that the overwhelming majority of guys, when the interviewers approached them and said, "Hey, would you talk about Vietnam," that it was the first time they ever openly and fully discussed their feelings.

TRUSCOTT: Probably a lot of times it was the first time they'd told anybody they were a veteran.

MULLER: When you compare the statistics that have come in, saying close to 80 percent of Vietnam veterans have never really talked about their experiences, you then realize how fortunate, I think, and unique the Vietnam Veterans Against the War experience was.

But this all goes to the whole thing: Where is the Vietnam veteran, and are we represented? The activists in the Vietnam veteran community that relate to veterans' organizations, to veteran issues and forums and symposiums, are, by and large, clearly left-wing, antidraft, antimilitary, angry guys. But that is not the whole population. What will be the consensus amongst the majority who we haven't heard from I don't know. What I'd like to say is that Vietnam—the experience and the issues—is too often looked at in terms of black and white and, for me, clearly, you cannot deal with any of this stuff in a superficial way. It is the gray. It is my roommate from basic school in the Marine Corps who served also as an infantry platoon commander and when I said, "Kevin, why don't you join me in speaking out against the war?" he said, "Bobby, I agree with you but I wrote to 26 mothers whose sons were killed under my command and I cannot publicly acknowledge that their deaths were for nothing." It's that kind of push-pull that makes any simple reduction in the statement of where these guys are coming from the wrong thing to do. I think it's remarkable that VVAW still stands to this day, in my opinion, as the only viable representation of the Vietnam veteran community. There has not been another organization that has been able to say and speak with any authority that it represents a broad base of Vietnam veterans.

WEBB: Well, I'd like to disagree with that, very respectfully.

MULLER: Jump in.

WEBB: You know, I never met a member of VVAW until I came up on the Hill in '77, and I've been around an awful lot of people that I served with and classmates of mine, etcetera. In talking to people who had active positions in VVAW, as near as I can figure there were never more than 7,000 Vietnam veterans in the organization totally. And what they said, although they had the right to say it, never represented my emotions about Vietnam. And again, I think, when you're talking about how representative are we, perhaps we should also talk about how representative have been the issues that have been addressed over the years, and these symbolic events. For instance, Vietnam Veterans Against the War. That's a symbolic organization. They purported to speak for a lot of people. They did focus a lot of attention on the plight of the Vietnam veterans, to their credit. We talk about Kent State. One of the great ironies to me when we look at Kent State is that for years people in Ohio, in that area, have been attempting to get a monument erected to that accident—and that's the way I view it, as an accident, perhaps even an inevitable accident. Four people died at Kent State in an accident and a community wants to use that as a symbolic event that represents what went on in Vietnam. And the proposed monument is an older person with a dagger pointing at a younger person who is dying. That supposedly is Vietnam. The generation gap. And I just wonder how many of Ohio's citizens died in Vietnam and I wonder how many monuments there are, either existing or recommended, to the people of Ohio who died under other conditions.

"I'll never forget how I wanted to just scream out of that ambulance, 'People! There's a war going on! Right now, guys are dying in firefights. Ambushes are being triggered. There's a war going on!'"

—Robert Muller

HARWOOD: I was interested to hear Phil's comment about sitting in the restaurant because I remember when I came back from the war in 1946 I felt the same way. A uniform was a dime a dozen and all I felt, particularly when I landed in the States, in San Diego, is all those people wanted to do was get me drunk and roll me or get my money or use me in some way. So the rage I don't find unique to this bunch. Out of every war, people are injured badly and a lot of them kill themselves. That's not unique. But I do have a feeling there is something unique about this, and that's what I'm trying to get at. And I'd like to throw one little thing out that I read: that in World War II you went in, number one, for the duration. Number two, you were assigned to a unit—I was with the same unit virtually during four years. Number three, when you came home, you came home on a boat, you had a couple of months and all you could talk about with your pals that you'd been with for four years was what you were going to do and what a bunch of assholes everybody in the service was, blah, blah, blah. Whereas in Vietnam, everybody in the officer class went over there and got his ticket punched in 13 months and then came home. The troops only served 12 months. They came over, as I understand it, in replacement battalions or something like that.

WHEELER: Individually.

HARWOOD: And one day you're at Khe Sanh, and the next day you're on a 737 flying back to San Francisco, and in a week you're back home in civilian clothes. The theory of this man was that there was no opportunity for the kind of therapeutic conversations that you mentioned, Bobby, that you'd never found anybody you could talk to. And I think several of you people have indicated that it just isn't there. There's no forum, no kindred spirit who can listen to you and know what you're talking about. Is that true?

MULLER: There is, I'm sure, a factor there, on the nature of the decompression period and all of that. But if you want to know what the rage is in me, let me just give you a sense of it without having brought my thoughts on this together. I'm just going to run it right through.

Marines were used like fucking cannon fodder in Vietnam. There were more U.S. Marine casualties in Vietnam than there were U.S. Marine casualties in the entire Second World War. When I was in training they told us that 60 percent of enlisted guys in line units were casualties. You're odds-on. Officers, it was 85 to 90 percent. I went out into the field with five other lieutenants, all of whom were Medevaced before me. In Vietnam I was on a patrol during the day or an ambush at night—every fucking day I was in country, with the exception of a couple. It was a war that was grinding in how they fucking inflicted casualties on us. I took over a platoon on the same day that it just had five guys killed and a whole shipful of guys wounded. I was out in the middle of fucking nowhere and we needed three choppers to be able to come in and get our company out. They said, "We can't spare the choppers. Walk out. Be advised, there are two NVA [North Vietnamese army] battalions sweeping through your area." Three days, morning before the sun rose till sunset, we marched, basically Indian file, down a river, because it was the only way you could negotiate the jungle. Along the banks that were vertical, in three days we marched, waiting any second for the banks of the river to open and just take us all out. We used to patrol and see a big garrison NVA flag flying right over the DMZ [Demilitarized Zone—the border between North and South Vietnam]. Couldn't touch it. I used to watch truck convoys at night coming down from North Vietnam. We used to have rules for engagement that were this thick about how we could fight the war, about when we could put a fucking magazine in the weapon.

WHEELER: Or couldn't fight the war.

MULLER: We had the people that were supposedly there to help being the same people that were fucking with us in ambushes and sniping at us and so forth. The frustration in fighting the war is a very real source of rage, in and of itself.

To come home: I remember my first time out of the hospital was to go from the naval hospital to the veterans' hospital. They took me by ambulance at 8 o'clock in the morning in New York and I was stunned with the rush-hour traffic. I said, "Holy shit, it's business as usual." Life goes on. Everybody's going to work. And I'll never forget how I wanted to just scream out of that ambulance, "People! There's a war going on! Right now, guys are dying in firefights. Ambushes are being triggered. There's a war going on!" Business as usual.

I go to the veterans' hospital and get this GS-5 shucking and jivin' and giving me a ration of shit because I need a pitcher of water, because I can't get out of bed. I get a society that cavalierly dismisses the war and deals with it as abstract fucking rhetoric. It wasn't an abstraction, it wasn't an intellectual reasoning process—were we right or were we wrong?—it's real. You took me out of my fucking life. You destroyed my fiancée. You put my parents through turmoil. You caused my brother to have an almost emotional breakdown in dealing with everything that happened. And you were very cavalier about the whole thing. Business as usual.

This is not just one other concern of the day. This *is* the concern. To have leaders that sent us to war abandon us, all those policymakers, all those politicians. Where were they to champion our cause? 1972: Fucking Richard Nixon vetoed the Veterans' Medical Care Expansion Act the week before the election as inflationary. "It's fiscally irresponsible," to quote his veto message. I called in $100,000 a day destroying fucking villages and killing people. And now to get me in that shithole VA hospital where I was put in bed with fucking drunks and derelicts and degenerates and old fucking has-beens, to call it "fiscally irresponsible" and inflationary to give us two sets of fucking parallel bars instead of one? A set of graduated steps? Some sense of privacy in the fucking enema rooms? You want to talk about a sense of rage? I could go on, but you're getting my drift.

FALLOWS: When you were going through the rush-hour traffic and you wanted to tell the people, "There's a war going on," what did you want them to then say? The other place where you heard that same sort of stuff was—with all the caveats of inauthenticity and paternalism and everything else—at the colleges. That's where people were saying, "Look, you have to stop the classes, the war is going on. It has to stop." What did you want the people to say when you said, "The war is going on"? Did you want them to stop the war? Did you want them to recognize your experience? What?

CAPUTO: Recognize that something was happening. I think that what Bobby's talking about is some sense of acknowledgment of the reality that all of us experienced over there.

There is a kind of myth that has grown up, mostly within military circles and certainly within those veteran circles from, say, World War II, about this "limited tour" business. "We were in there for the duration. You guys were in there for a year." Like we were off in day camp. When I was writing *Rumor*, I was looking at old unit diaries. And I asked a friend of mine, Dave Quinlan, who is now a lieutenant colonel in the Marine historical archives, to give me a list of the Marine casualties in Vietnam. And I looked at it and the total casualties came to 105,000, which is 15,000 over the total casualties in World War II. And I said, "Jesus!" you know, because I grew up—you hear "Iwo Jima" and you see all these battalions falling down like wheat. And he said what few people realized was that the only valid comparison, as far as what he called man combat hours went, was the trench warfare of World War I.

And what Bobby said was damn true, that when you went out in the bush you stayed there, and you would go out, say on a major op, battalion-size or something, you'd spend five or six days slogging around out there and maybe one operation we're on we hit a really hot LZ [landing zone] and we took 75 or 80 casualties right off the bat. Then we got a dribble of casualties for the days after that. Slogging back, you went right back to the outpost that you'd been sitting on before you went on the operation. You went back to the goddam patrol and the next day you go out and patrol and, boom, another mine goes off and another guy's gone. And you were in a state of mental alert. Tremendous tension for as long as you were in the bush.

And I think, in a sense, it was worse on junior officers, even though junior officers would only spend seven or eight or nine months in the bush. Some did their whole 13. But you had a responsibility, I'd say, if you were a platoon commander or a squad leader, that was much greater than in previous conflicts because the war was so individual. I remember when I was on this outpost forward of what we used to call "the main line of resistance," which was just a bunch of other outposts with huge holes in between them. We were out there 2,000 meters forward of anybody. And all alone. Just completely all alone. Just me and my platoon—to the point where we used to look at the other platoons in our company like they came from some strange tribe in New Guinea. You almost didn't even have a sense of connection with them.

You would have this sense of responsibility. I know I did. And I'm sure any platoon commander would. Every night that I was on that outpost I'd look at that damn thing and I'd say, "This position is untenable." And I remember there was bush growing almost right up to the wire. I used to call back and I'd say, "Can I get some flames out here to burn this stuff off?" I said, "I have zero fields of fire, because I've got infiltrators that can just come right up here and throw a golf ball in the post." And I always got, "No, we can't, because that little patch of jungle surrounds this old Cao Dai temple which is sacred to the people of the village," and all that. And, sure enough, it happened one night. I was sleeping in my bunker and, wham, off goes the grenade. Fortunately, nobody was hurt. And it was that kind of experience that began to develop that anger in me. That feeling of being not a soldier serving a cause, but of a pawn serving a policy—and a policy which, moreover, seemed to change every day. Or which not even the leaders who were running the policy could articulate themselves.

And when I look back on it, the incident when I sent those guys out into that village and I had said, "We've got this info that they're VC sappers," and I said, "Capture them and if they give you any trouble, waste those motherfuckers." Which is what they then did. But there was that rage doing it. There was that feeling of: I'm out here trying to save my own life and trying to save the lives of these 33 guys who are under me and I'm serious about this war. I'm really serious about it, because it's my young ass that's on the line. And in a way, that was sort of showing them how serious I was about it. And I think that that anger carried through and then became aggravated by all the things that Bobby talked about. The sense of total misunderstanding, misjudgment of what you're up to.

WEBB: I think all men who undergo combat feel alienated when they return to their society. The difference is that previously there has been a form of catharsis once you come back. It has been a catharsis that was generated from your community to the individual. When I was in Vietnam the 1st Marine Division, on any given day, had a thousand activities going and they were all going in a different direction. The sort of responsibility and pressure on the squad leaders and platoon commanders was really enormous. That also created a by-product, once a person had gone through this, of a great amount of pride. He felt like he had done something very meaningful. When he came back, he had expectations.

Again, some distinctions between World War II and Vietnam: nature of operations, length of service. In World War II, people enlisted for the duration. Even when I got up on the Veterans' Committee in 1977, the feeling about people who had served in Vietnam was, "Well, they were draftees, they did their 18 months, they got out, they did not suffer a very severe interruption." The average Vietnam-era veteran served 34 months, in the time period when we were talking about "future shock" and also in a military system where he was a minority of his age group being pulled away from his community. So he suffered very severe disruptions. The average World War II veteran served 30 months. The average World War I veteran served 12 months.

And we have never recognized the nature of Vietnam service. Two thirds of the people who went into the service during Vietnam were volunteers. Two thirds of the people who went in during World War II were drafted. The nature of your peer group, too: 16 million people during World War II were in uniform. So when you were coming back, your expression that a uniform was worth a dime was very true. Less than 9 million people out of a much larger group over an extended period of time wore uniforms in Vietnam and uniforms were not only worth a dime, they were not worth a damn.

The nature of the war itself: To give you a direct analogy, the 2nd Marine Division—the Battle Cry Division which was on Tarawa, which was on Saipan and which I admire greatly—was in the South Pacific a total of three years. They were in combat a total of six weeks. When they were in, it was brutal. Tarawa was a 79-hour mad moment. But when they got away from it they could go down to Australia. They could get drunk, they could get laid, they could refurbish, they could become human beings again. They could work this out as they were going through it, as well. In Vietnam the Marine Corps, as Bobby and Phil both made clear, operated continually. We didn't see barbed wire for 80 days at a time. And what they would do because of manpower constraints was enormous. I had one guy who was shot between the eyes. It went in right here as a dime and came out down here as a quarter. He spent three months in a Japanese hospital and they sent him right back to us. As a matter of fact, he was wounded twice. It took us a couple of hours to get him out and he was hurt by a B-40 round going out. Can you imagine what that guy's mental state was by the time he got back to us again? Then, coming home, 95 percent of the people that I knew and that I talked to felt good on a very personal level about what they had done when they were in Vietnam. But they had an inability to catharsize their community because of the inundation of the media. This was the first real media war. People lost their curiosity about the experience. So a person was left to deal with it alone. The statistic that 80 percent of the people had never talked about it, I found that going around doing radio shows. I'll do call-in shows and I'll get people who for the first time ever are talking about it. And you can feel it in their voices. There's a true sense of isolation. And I think it's the coupling that's been so important when you talk about the experience. It's not just the sense of alienation or even the sense of rage, it's having nothing, nowhere to vent it. No way to be brought back into the community on the terms of the experience. And so the rage sort of erodes from the inside out.

TRUSCOTT: There's an obvious point that we're missing here, too, and that is that every other war that this country has fought was identifiable collectively and individually as having been won, and this war was never identified as being won. This war was lost. It wasn't won. It was lost. So we can sit here and talk from now until doomsday about lack of support in the field, and basically how fucked up everything was, and how they would spend 100 grand a day on artillery shells or whatever and not a nickel in a VA hospital. But veterans certainly expected the leadership of the country to respond in some way. And this is the way the leadership responded to VVAW: They infiltrated the leadership of VVAW with agents provocateurs. That's the way they reacted to the only veterans' group that did anything other than have a parade and wave some flags on Memorial Day. And the way that the leadership reacted to the entire matter of the war by 1971 was called Vietnamization, and it was reducing the number of guys who were there. The whole time I was working for *The Village Voice* I was for the bombing of the North. I figured as long as you're going to have one guy in combat in Vietnam, just one American over there, the last guy, they ought to be calling in every fucking penny's worth of fire that they can call in for the guy.

"A lot of men were chewed up by the war experience, some were killed, but if the heat in the oven is higher, the steel that comes out has got to be better."

—John Wheeler

WHEELER: I'd like to mark something. I don't think it's going to do our country any good for us to do what we can do to a perfection of legal satisfaction, to prove that we are a screwed minority. We were stuck in the ass, all of us. I think we have to identify it, but I think the work on that score is something we're going to have to handle ourselves, up on the cross all by ourselves, just like you said in your book, Phil. But if we could establish—and maybe we already have—that the war was unique, for a whole vector of reasons, I think that by the same token we are unique, because of the pressure. A lot of men were chewed up by the war experience, some were killed, but if the heat in the oven is higher, the steel that comes out has got to be better. And I want to affirm something: that out of that process, and out of eating our own death—and we're doing it by ourselves, frankly, betrayed by the generation ahead of us—I think the challenge that lies before us is not to get ourselves set up as some kind of superminority, one more special-interest group, but, instead, to figure out what it is we have to offer. And I think the heat was higher and we do have something special to offer out there.

And there's an example and it's you, Bobby Muller. When I met you—do you remember the night?—you were saying, "God-damn, there's going to be a Vietnam Veterans of America," and you said, "Now, what are we going to do?" And what did I say? Three years ago. I said, "Bobby, you're going to be a leader." And what did *Time* magazine do a year ago? Out of 50 young American leaders, how many Vietnam vets? Who? Robert Muller! See what I'm getting at? Chop off his legs, you know, and you bring him back and the rats crawl over his bed, OK, and what do you get? You get a sign. The sign is that there is unique leadership capability. Our job while we're up on the cross, and we are, every one of us, is to eat the death all by ourselves. There's too many guys in the older generation that walked away. And there are too many guys in our own generation who don't understand how the war shaped them, unlike Jim Fallows. We who were in the combat zone—especially you who were out in the bush for more days of engagement with a hostile force than has ever happened since the First World War—we have to get over that and eat it ourselves and give what we've got to our country because I think the damn country needs it. And not only that, we've got to convince the other 57 million people in our generation of what it is we have to offer and get somebody to give us a chance to start carrying out our mission. There's a lot of positive that can come out of the experience.

CAPUTO: There certainly is. But there is a reluctance that borders on a kind of retirement about Vietnam veterans, it seems to me, becoming leaders.

TRUSCOTT: A reluctance to reembrace leadership.

CAPUTO: And I don't know how that's going to be overcome. Jim's got a perfect background for it. He's a lawyer, lives here in Washington, lots of medals. If he had been in World War II, at the age he's now at he would be in the public limelight, he would be running for some office. And his decorations, his war experience would be great pluses. Tomorrow, if Jim declared his candidacy for some office and he got up and he said the things that he said or implied in his book, that "I was there," that "I served, and I'm proud of what I did," I maintain that he wouldn't have a snowball's chance in hell. The only way right now that a Vietnam veteran can become a leader in the political sense of the term is that he does the self-flagellation number: "Oh, I was there and it was so terrible and so awful and I'm so sorry for burning the villages and please forgive me."

And that attitude still prevails, I think, within the "establishment" within this country and until the time comes that somebody does analogously what we've done here ... I mean, these books broke the ice. Until these books were published, that subject was as anathema as pornography was in the Victorian era. I'm not kidding you. My editor told me that when she first got the manuscript, she wouldn't look at it for two weeks. Wouldn't even read it. And until this kind of thing happens on a national political level, we're not going to see that leadership because these guys are going to be afraid of being, if you will, hurt again.

WHEELER: Well, there's one thing about leadership that Lucian put his finger on and it's the thing I treasure in his book. He says one thing about leadership, he says it's the special secret: You've got to be willing to die for your men. Now, that suggests sacrifice and an intimate knowledge of what sacrifice means. And if you can think analytically about what it is that we would carry out of the furnace of our experience, I think one of them is that kind of gut-level knowledge of sacrifice and how you weave it into the fabric of policy. And maybe, to give you a precise answer, there are two kinds of politics: There's elective politics but there's also something just as important called appointive politics. And maybe the shrewd senior presidential appointee or the president himself can figure out that there's a line of attributes that runs among certain men like Jim that says, "That's the right man for the job." And, to pick one example that may be a hopeful sign, there is a guy most of you know, Joe Zengerle, who helped Bobby get the organization that Bobby's got started. Joe is now an assistant secretary of the Air Force and five years ago they would have said "Joseph Zengerle? Appoint him? That's a fox watching the chickens." But we're beginning to learn that if you're going to buy a lot of weapons that they have to be simple, easy to maintain, you need someone who understands—to use the phrase someone said—"the chemistry of the line unit." So if you say I'm grasping for straws you're right, but still I think that promise is there.

CAPUTO: I think that the veterans of the war do have a lot to contribute to the country and on a political leadership level, and I think that it is sorely needed right now. It's probably dangerous to speak in such generalizations, but I tend to think that people who were in Vietnam are much more clearheaded about what needs to be done to get this country, which I feel—it's the conventional wisdom now—is in a mess.

And I think there's another qualification and that is that

Vietnam veterans, having served in such a brutal and futile conflict, would be—despite the public image of them being warriors and bloodthirsty—actually would be much more reluctant and much less cavalier about saying, "Oh, well, let's send a battalion into Lower Volta," or something like that. I think they would be much more clearheaded about what to do. I think they would be much more judicious in making that decision, because they know what it was like. They didn't, like Carter, float around in a nuclear submarine in peacetime. But I think that, once having made that decision, they would say to themselves, "All right, now what can we do to make this operation successful?" In other words, "Let's win it." Which obviously, as far as our foreign policy goes right now, is absolutely crucial.

WEBB: I think one of the clearest manifestations of that is the recent interview with Army Col. Charles Beckwith on this aborted Iran hostage rescue raid. We all have our opinions about whether and how and why and everything else, but when Beckwith was asked, rather patronizingly, I thought, "Couldn't you have been just a good soldier and taken those five helicopters and gone on in?" he looked at the guy who asked him and said, "With all due respect, you don't know where you're coming from." Anybody who has pointed his finger and seen somebody drop at his behest, that will never leave him. And it is a very good thing to have.

But I would like to be just a bit more optimistic, I think, than either of you are. Some of these things have a way of working themselves out. We are in a watershed time in this country and I think that people are starting to look around for new answers, and when they look around for new answers they're going to be looking for new role models. I think what the people are going to be looking for is individuals who have manifested a sense of country. We are advancing out of this notion of dissent being the only way to deal with policy and we're getting into looking for more affirmative approaches. Again, without being patronizing, I think that Jim Fallows has manifested an enormous sense of country and of attempting to come to grips with these things without regard to putting ego first or self-image first. Those sorts of people are just as important as our sorts of people.

TRUSCOTT: What you've been talking about has been a process of rebuilding. I think there's more personal rebuilding going on, and more success at it, among Vietnam veterans than there is among the 18 million guys who didn't go. Because all these people have been sitting around living with the idea that they dodged the draft or they got out or they paid their thousand bucks and got their dental work; they've been living with that for 15 years now. They need to hear what it is that Vietnam veterans have to offer so that, to be trite, each side can sort of stop hating the other one. I mean, there's all this rage and hatred and I can guarantee you, and I think Jim Fallows can guarantee you, that there's people who have the idea that they exercised a strong sense of duty and country and honor by opposing the war. And people who have the idea that they played a major part in helping to stop the war were just as angry during that time that the fucking war was going on as anybody else was, so there's different kinds of a sense of having served one's country.

The other thing that I'd like to address here is that there's an extraordinary amount of responsibility for what goes on in the military leadership in this country itself. If you go back and look at people's careers and where people are now: Who are the guys who are running the Army and the Navy and the Air Force and the Marines? Who's the chief of staff? Who was the last chief of staff? Who was the one before that? Who's DCSPER [deputy chief of staff for personnel]? Who are all these guys? They made a conscious decision as far back as 1966 and '67 that that fucking war was going in the toilet and they started grooming guys who had one year over there as whole colonels and kept their asses stateside. Bernie Rogers is a perfect example. He was an assistant division commander over there and then came back and was statesided and cushioned and protected along, so that by the time the war was over and so forth he could become a decent chief of staff that nobody was going to get real upset about, because he wasn't going to be a Col. Beckwith as a chief of staff. He wasn't going to be some no-neck gorilla in there that says, "Now, I did 40 tours and I'm going to chew nails and eat tacks and fire the shit out of you." No, they needed Clean-for-Gene types and they started grooming those types back that far and, as far as I'm concerned, that's reprehensible.

WHEELER: Do you know who'd love that? The Soviet general staff. They'd love it!

TRUSCOTT: It's reprehensible and it's also an acknowledgment, a tacit kind of acknowledgment, of the military leadership itself stopping being leaders.

MULLER: What we're talking about is not history. What we're talking about is today. And who's running the military today is a continuance of who was running the military back then. Part of the rage was: Vietnam offered many different kinds of experiences for the soldiers. I went through a large number of them. It differed as to where you were geographically and when you were there. I was there in '68. I operated primarily in northern I Corps. And I did go from the Highlands, through the villes, and so on and so forth. And I also worked with the ARVN, the South Vietnamese. Part of my sense of rage was: any guy who was in the field had to know that a "McNamara line" was a concept generated thousands of miles from where we were. An electronic barrier to prevent infiltration where we were was absurd. And yet they tried to perpetuate the farce that this is a technological barrier that's going to win the war. The writing was on the wall.

I served as an adviser to three separate ARVN battalions, every one of which, every time we were in combat, split. Not most of the time, every time! Goddamn it, the day I got blown away, I had a suicide squad left of NVA that were dug in on a hilltop—16 to 20 guys max, and they held off me, 500 fucking ARVN, 10 U.S. Marine tanks, an hour and a half heavy artillery prep, two flame tanks, everything. All right. They're tough motherfuckers. The Vietnamese, South, didn't want to fight. The writing was on the wall.

All right. I knew in 1968, as we were even starting to get out, there's no fucking way, without us being there in a very heavy-handed way, that we're going to turn that thing around. The eventual settlement of the Vietnam question was resolved. And yet, when we came back and we spoke and we gave testimony to what we'd experienced and what the reality of Vietnam was, as opposed to the crock of shit the politicians and the media were generating about what the reality of it was, we got infiltrated, we got called "the home-front snipers," and it was allowed to continue through '73 when every one of us that were there, that were in the real fighting capacities, knew that it was going down the tube. We gave our ass and we continued to give our ass, to save Richard Nixon's face. All right. And that's the cavalier manner that they used us, again, as the pawns as opposed to the fighting men.

WEBB: As you said, though, Bobby, realities varied.

MULLER: Yeah, but history proved me correct.

WEBB: I'm not sure history has proven anybody correct.

TRUSCOTT: History has a way of going on and on and on.

MULLER: But the questions that were raised by that are the questions that are still there today. We had—in my opinion, admittedly, a systemic failure with Vietnam. We had a failure on the part of the military to properly assess the situation and to implement the conduct of a war policy that could lead to a success. The failure of the military, added to the abdication of the Congress, the excesses of the office of the presidency, the effect of the media on the public and what that does to continuing the base of support for a war effort are questions which have not been, I don't think, objectively looked at, with the lessons understood and appreciated by the public. What is to prevent, however well intentioned it may be, for our involvement in another part of the world at some point in the future, those same systemic failures from repeating themselves?

WHEELER: Bobby, they repeated themselves in the Iranian desert.

MULLER: What have we done so that we know that the officer is not going to give the report to his senior that his senior wants to hear, instead of giving him a report about what's really going down?

The response to us when we said all of that was a continuing sense of rage. The Marine Corps motto is Semper Fidelis— Always Faithful. In Vietnam we went back for the wounded, we went back for the dead. There was a very heavy sense of responsibility for our men on the part of each of us that are here. Where are those fucking officers that were above us? Where are the leaders? Where are the politicians that sent us to war? I can't get in to see Clark Clifford, Robert McNamara. I can't see these jokers. They don't even want to even think about hearing about what it is that I'm trying to say on behalf of Vietnam veterans. I cannot raise money. I cannot raise support. I cannot even get in to see the Clark Cliffords, the Rostows, anybody. The total fucking abandonment of those people that sent us to the fucking war is unbelievable!

All of this has come together with that Harris survey that shows America has repudiated the Vietnam War, that the majority of the public considers the Vietnam veterans, to use Harris's phrase, "to have been made the sucker for their having served."

WHEELER: Bobby, can't you do it yourself? Why do you need McGeorge Bundy and Clark Clifford?

MULLER: Jack, why you need the leadership is not only for the public at large but the Vietnam veterans. The Vietnam veterans don't want to come together around their status as a Vietnam veteran. They don't want to identify as a Vietnam veteran. Why? Because, why should you? When you do, you are, to go back to a somewhat dated stereotype that was laid on us, "the killer of women and children." Indiscriminate. The Lieutenant Calley syndrome. The public reacted to us this way. You were a junkie. All right? You were the crazed psychopath portrayed on the police melodramas. Or, perhaps most damaging to a lot of guys, you're the dummy. You cannot get Vietnam veterans to come together. They want to forget it, they want to stay away from it. They don't want to come together on the basis of something that's a big negative. You're not going to be able to organize Vietnam veterans. You're not going to get the manifestation and the expression of the leadership that they have the opportunity and ability to present until you clean it up, man. They're not coming together.

TRUSCOTT: An even more shocking point would be, you can't get those people who were the leaders of the soldiers during the Vietnam War, who were themselves Vietnam veterans, like the chief of staff or guys that were division commanders, you can't get them together. How come the chief of staff of the Army or the chairman of the Joint Chiefs, how come he wasn't recognized by *Time* magazine as the leading advocate for the Vietnam veteran in this country? Those guys commanded them. They were the ones who led them. Or why not, just like you said, why not Clark Clifford, why not the secretary of defense? Why have the leaders of the recent past, the leaders during the war years, why have they deserted their duty to lead?

CAPUTO: I can tell, Bobby, that you've got something of a temper, and I don't want to incite it any more. Why do Vietnam veterans need to be organized in this formal way to begin with? I mean, isn't it true that some of these problems, whether individual or collective, will work themselves out by themselves? I don't understand. Don't take this in the wrong way, but, frankly, you're starting to sound to me like a union organizer. And I don't see why we've got to say, quote unquote, "the International Brotherhood of Vietnam Veterans." I mean, what is that going to do?

MULLER: I'll give you a simple answer....

WEBB: Wait a minute, you've given a half hour of simple answers....Well, go ahead, then. But don't take a half hour this time.

MULLER: When Carter came into office, Zengerle—the one that Jack mentioned, he was the law clerk to Chief Justice Burger—he did a survey. Carter had 700 policymaking appointments in the Civil Service Commission list, the "plum book." Five went to Vietnam veterans, out of 700. At the same time, hundreds of our nonveteran peers—the activists, if you wish, of the '60s—are represented in the Carter administration in a very significant number. Well over a hundred, at least. OK. In politics, networking is the key. Who you know. You give each other a leg up. You factor in your sensitivities and your concerns into the decision-making process. In the *Bakke* decision, we didn't have Vietnam veterans in policymaking positions in Justice or whatever to argue the point: "Hey, this guy is as old as he is because he spent four years in the Marines, because he was there because of the Vietnam War." You've got to be able to factor into decision making, into policymaking, the sensitivities and concerns of your constituents. When we are not represented, it's hard to do.

WHEELER: Bobby, let's say that it wasn't five but you could make it 30, which is a modest improvement. What is it that they can do?

MULLER: What they can do is factor in our recent experience into the policy issues and the questions of the day. Namely, most notably right now, military manpower requirements. The volunteer army isn't making it. We're talking about a draft. The fundamental question: Who should serve? I think, goddamn it, we have a lot of experience and something to say about that question. The hand-in-hand question to me is: Who makes the decision as to when that military is going to be committed? All sorts of questions: Who should serve? What is the obligation of a citizen to serve? How do you distribute the burden of wartime service among the population? Who makes the decisions to commit?

WHEELER: Could I suggest just one more question? And that is this: Is liberty worth dying for?

MULLER: Well, if the last group that did it are considered suckers for having tried it, I don't think you're going to have much success getting another generation to respond.

"I don't know what the methodology of reconciliation is or, for that matter, if there really is such a thing, but I know what I would like to do....I would like one day to put my arms around this

Elizabeth McAlister or Philip Berrigan and even Tom Hayden, for that matter, and literally say that we—all of us—went through something together."
—Philip Caputo

FALLOWS: It seems to me the real goal of hashing this stuff out again is to do for the generation as a whole what I think has started to be done in the last couple of years for the Vietnam veterans: of talking through the things that have been really bothersome and, by exposing them, making them less damaging and less dangerous. I want to try to explain a little bit of how the things I think are on the minds of a lot of people like me who, unlike all the rest of you, weren't in the Army those days.

The first thing is, it seems to me that we have this flow chart of where people ended up. There are Vietnam veterans, 3 million or so. I think there are probably 3 or 5 million people on the other side, men, for whom not being in the Army remains as emotionally significant a thing as having been in the Army was for all of you. I think there are probably another 10 or 15 million for whom not being in the Army then was like not being in the Army now—I mean, it's not a major, shaping part of their lives. So I think we're talking about not the preponderance of the people of our vintage, but clusters on each side who felt and feel still shaped by the experience.

As I look back on those times, there are three different strands that seem to me present among the people I knew and the proportion of those things in different people I think affects the way you feel now. The first of those elements, which I still believe very deeply, was a sense of loyalty to country and exercising your duty to your country by opposing the war. There was that indisputable element of sincere opposition. I still think that it was the correct thing to try to oppose the war and that that is one point of pride, if you will, that people still feel that it was the correct thing to do—not to oppose the people involved in it but to oppose the policy itself.

The second element was the way that first part got tainted and polluted by a sense of anti-Americanism and anti-servicemanism. And I think that those people who were most under the sway of this second element, of anti-Americanism and hating the service-man, are the ones who are now most reluctant to think about these days, because they realize now in general, I think, that that was an excess of the times, that it was wrong. One sidelight on this point: At the beginning of this week I was out in Youngstown, Ohio. They were having a big debate in Youngstown about the draft and they couldn't find anybody in the country to go support the draft, so I was up there supporting the draft and debating this Elizabeth McAlister, Philip Berrigan's wife, who had this 30-minute speech about "We won't die for your lies anymore," and...

TRUSCOTT: "We," she said?

FALLOWS: Yeah, "we."

TRUSCOTT: Cute.

FALLOWS: She seemed to represent this anti-Americanism and anti-servicemanism in a pure unchanged form.

TRUSCOTT: That's called a freeze-dried liberal.

FALLOWS: The people who were most like her in those years are the ones who are going to be most reluctant to make a peace with people like you, because they feel the most uneasiness about that.

I think the third significant thing about people of my sort in that time was the convenient fact, rather than the motivating factor, that the pursuit of these critical opinions you had also meant not being in combat yourself. It was the fact that you didn't want people to go to the war, therefore you didn't want yourself to go to the war. And that meant that all the people who were protesting ended up finding ways to get out of the draft. As I say, it was a convenient fact rather than the causing fact. But the result is that you have a great preponderance of people who did not lay themselves on the line by resisting the draft formally, going to prison or whatever, or by being in combat, and who have very mixed feelings about that. And I think that, too, is another barrier toward getting these things talked about with some openness. There is this whole area where people have, I think, the standard psychoanalytic problems from actions that they partly understand and partly feel proud about but partly feel guilty about, and you see the backlash of this in the people who are now signing up for the reserves or are supermilitarists or whatever. But I think that it is important to recognize this psyche in those who took a different path from you, in doing whatever we can to repair the breach.

And just to pursue this for a second, I think most of my college and graduate school friends are not happy talking about these things because they're afraid they're going to be yelled at. They're afraid that all of you are going to shake them by the lapels and say, "You fucking coward! You weren't there with us." And that is why they don't want to talk about this stuff. They would then say, "Well, you fucking war criminal!"

TRUSCOTT: I've been around a long time and I've never heard that. I've never heard a guy, a vet, go to an antiwar guy and say, "You're a coward." I've never heard that.

FALLOWS: I think that maybe the fear is partly unrealistic, partly self-inflicted, but I think I have some experience in this vein, having written about this and having a fair collection of letters. Most of it is not from veterans. I find them usually less willing to judge than other people. There is a substantial constituency in this country that's going to say, "You fucking coward." I have letters from about 4,000 of them. About half of them are women, usually our parents' vintage. It's mainly the wives of veterans, their fathers, their mothers, and that's more or less it.

WHEELER: Why do the women do that?

FALLOWS: You got me.

TRUSCOTT: You know, women have been touched by the experience of the war, they've been touched in ways that I don't completely understand because there hasn't been enough dialogue about it. Every girl that went with a guy for those 10 years that we're talking about got touched by whatever kind of personal experience that guy went through—whatever kind of torment each one of those 27 million went through to decide yes, no, or "I'm going to dodge," or "I'm not" or lucking out or whatever. So they all got touched and it's something that's got a broad, sweeping effect on them, not to mention their mothers, the women's mothers and the women's fathers.

WEBB: I hope we won't lose one of the points that Jim made. The overriding question to me is the question of societal values and where you place such things as an obligation to a culture. One thing they used to ask us all the time at the Naval Academy was, "Are you bigger than yourself?" There are things that are larger than an individual, that he owes his allegiance to, or else a culture does not have any momentum. Is it your experience that the people who merely found a sense of convenience in this issue, but, as you point out, are reluctant to address the issue, is it also your experience that they are reluctant to provide a forum? Is there a censorship, an unwitting censorship as far as even addressing these issues in a way that someone else will be able to come to resolution with them?

FALLOWS: Let me answer that in a little different way. I was trying to suggest that each one of these three motives is present in differing degrees. All of them were present but the proportions were different for different people. So, at the time, I think, there was in almost all the people at least a modicum of this feeling that they were doing their duty too, and the problem now is that, because there were also these other elements which most of them look back on with some chagrin, with some shame, that most people have not been able to honestly sort out the things they should be proud about and advertise as values to their children, to other people, and the things they should honestly regret. And so it is the unspoken and unanalyzed nature of these things which I think is the big roadblock to your knowing more of those people and their being willing to hear what you have to say.

CAPUTO: There are very few people that get all of that out for themselves right up front. That's why at this table right now there's a whole bunch of writers sitting around and not a whole bunch of stockbrokers.

FALLOWS: And there are all these novels about the experience you all have had and almost no honest writing about the other side. There are more of you who have thrashed out these things in a public way so you're known as having dealt with them than there are of my sort. And that, I think, is a symptom.

TRUSCOTT: Count the books on the war at home. Those books would fill two shelves in a library. Every single thing about the antiwar movement was celebrated, celebrated again and then recelebrated until finally you're about ready to puke.

FALLOWS: But I look on those the way you would look on a book about Vietnam that celebrated the wonderful assaults here and there. It doesn't really tell you...

TRUSCOTT: No, I don't look upon the books with derision. I look on them as a body of work that was salable in the same way that all of a sudden women's books became salable.

FALLOWS: I want to go back to Jim Webb's book, which is a work of fiction that I greatly admire. It also is, I think, especially because of the ending, something that is almost designed to anger and threaten the other side, who thinks, "Well, here is a guy who's calling us fucking cowards." That's certainly your right to do, but I think it is worth each side's understanding the other. And that's all I'm saying here, that the only point in the long run is to try to understand what's on each other's minds, if there is going to be anything but this real gulf.

WEBB: There is nothing in my book that calls anybody a coward.

TRUSCOTT: You know, one of the problems we face here today is a problem that we faced much more profoundly 10 years ago, 15 years ago. When I went to West Point in '65, I was conservative and there was nothing I wanted to be more in my whole life than an Army officer. And these values that were held up to us as a guidon in those days I see nothing wrong with. I've never seen anything wrong with an honor code that says you shouldn't lie, cheat or steal. So there's nothing wrong with "Duty, Honor, Country." But when you start to see those values perverted... When I was 22 years old I was pretty well convinced from having officer after officer after officer—major, lieutenant colonel, full colonel—come and tell me, personally or in front of a class, "You've got to go to Vietnam and get your fucking ticket punched. The war sucks. It's full of it. It's a suck-ass war. We're

not going to win it. We're not fighting it right, but go and do it."
You know, "Duty, Honor, Country" had suddenly become "Self-duty, Honor, Country." And I didn't make it that. I was a graduate of that.

WEBB: That was an individual decision that everyone turned around and came to terms with on their own. We all come in from different referents and we all have different things that we cling to, and we're talking about a period that was filled with anguish and is gone with the exception of the leavings that are with us. And the key question again is, how are we going to resolve all these different sets of delusions, on the one hand, strong, clinging feelings, on the other, in a way that is going to allow us to address very real issues today?

TRUSCOTT: The word "reconciliation" is really, to me, the word that ought to be used, because it really opens the door that it's about time was opened. Any kind of reconciliation or resolving these differences has to take into account two things, at least. Just for starters. One, it has to take into account the honor of guys who went to Vietnam and guys who just went ahead and got drafted or were just drafted as victims of their own circumstance, and the fact that the serviceman was not a fool and an idiot but he was a man that served his country just like anybody ever did in any other year, and recognize their honor whether the war was won, lost or just left hanging. And, two, I think that any kind of reconciliation or resolving of that question has to take into consideration the honor of those people—and it's not an honor that's just in their heads, it was an honor that was reflected in the voting booths and everywhere else in this country, ultimately and eventually—of people who honestly and forthrightly and with a sense of honor opposed the war and took it as their duty as citizens to try to end the war. I really think that those two feelings are very, very close together.

WHEELER: When you say "honor," it's not a fashionable word. Could you read "integrity" for honor?

TRUSCOTT: Absolutely. People's own sense of personal worth. To be able to look at yourself in the mirror. To be able to live with yourself day after day. Now, I think that veterans are far and away ahead of the rest of the country in coming to grips with this stuff.

CAPUTO: I agree with you, by and large, but it's because veterans have had a much more intense experience that needed to be dealt with if they were to survive psychologically. Whatever conflicts are being undergone by these other 18 million, or whatever the number is, are not as intense nor as threatening. You had to get it settled out.

I don't know what the methodology of reconciliation is or, for that matter, if there really is such a thing, but I know what I would like to do, for all the sarcastic comments I've made about those sort of people. I would like one day to put my arms around this Elizabeth McAlister or Philip Berrigan and even Tom Hayden, for that matter, and literally say that we—all of us—went through something together.

FALLOWS: That none of us caused.

TRUSCOTT: Went through different kinds of hell.

CAPUTO: But on our part, it would have to take an effort of will. I can think of a concrete example of a very close friend of mine out west who is also a writer, who left the country to get out of the draft, to get out of the war, and who just told that to me one day. I mean, just about how desperate he was to escape the conscription and escape the war. And, as close as he was to me, when he said that my stomach just started to knot up. There wasn't even a moment's reflection and I just felt myself starting to tighten up. And that takes almost an effort of will, not to have that gut reaction. Having said that, I think that the burden of the reconciliation is more on the other side than it is on our side. Because they are the ones who were doing the criticizing. They are the ones who were the most strident and the most vocal and in many ways are the ones who did a lot, unconsciously or no, to undermine and destroy our sense of self-worth. I would really like to put my arm around them but I would like them not to say, "I'm putting my arm around you because you're a Vietnam veteran," and that sort of thing.

WHEELER: My guess is that because everything else you said is right, that when you get to the question of who has to reach out, I think it's the other way around. I just have this feeling that you've got to go to the person that's bleeding first to say, "I'd like to put my arm around you." And I think the reason that's true is because it's you who just said it. I didn't read Berrigan saying that.

CAPUTO: The way that this might develop, and I don't know that anything consciously could be done or programmatically could be done, but at some point in our history, within the near future, it is going to be realized that Vietnam was more than going to the war, just as Vietnam was a lot more than a lot of people carrying signs or NLF flags or whatever in the street, that this was a watershed in American history, perhaps nearly as big a one as the Civil War, and that we, all of us, shared in that wrenching experience. That all of us, if you will, are brothers and sisters in that sense and we have that in common. I must say that emotionally I feel that way every now and then when I run into a product of the '60s, although if this person happened to be very, very left or very radical or very against the war, that barrier exists anyhow. But it would be at some point where maybe we'd get a national leader—certainly one who is not on the horizon at the moment—like Lincoln, who actually talks about "charity toward all and malice toward none." And that breach is healed.

WEBB: I don't even know if we should be talking about burdens. I do not feel that the generation that came before us let us down. I do not feel put on by them. I think that the whole Vietnam period, first of all, if it was an error in our society, it was an error of good intentions. The dissent that rolled off of that rolled off for a number of reasons that were not peculiar to Vietnam. But I think that the bedrock, the one thing that we did get from the older generation, was a very strong sense of country. I think we all grew up with a very strong sense of country.

TRUSCOTT: I did.

WEBB: We all did. We started out with a sense of what this society's all about. In my opinion, this is the most creative society politically that has ever existed. We are a multicultured society, living side by side in a state of continuous abrasion. On any moral issue we are going to be at each other's throats, and that's beautiful, because it's creative, as long as we can sort of hold the outer fabric together. That's a starting point.

HARWOOD: The thing that fascinates me about this is that you really are our children. All these people, the progeny of the '60s, are our kids. What happened? I'm one of these confused elders. What the hell did we do wrong?

FALLOWS: To turn up us?

HARWOOD: Yeah. And I don't mean that in a pejorative way. I'm just saying that if you ever saw a bunch of traditional Americans it was us. And yet we spawned this thing, and I don't mean the young people but the whole thing. And in a sense we are responsible.

CAPUTO: One thing disturbs me when I hear people of your generation speak that way. There is something about your particular generation that tends to talk about, well, "My kid goes out and steals a car. What did I do wrong?" Well, maybe your kid's rotten. It may not have anything to do with you. I would very, very much hesitate to impose, over what I think is certainly a real division of emotion and of thought within the generation of which we are a part, a generational division that I don't think is real. It was a creation of the media, another way to simply explain an extraordinarily complex event which, moreover, is an event that has occurred throughout the 6,000 years of recorded history. Generations just happened to be different.

FALLOWS: It's not blaming a generation, but the fact is a historical tragedy, that an event occurred in which the very mixed strands of principle and loyalty in the country, and duty to military service, duty to your country's ideals or whatever, pulled people in different ways and ripped them asunder. So it was not somebody's fault. An event happened that inevitably ripped people apart like the Civil War and I think that's the heart of it.

HARWOOD: It seems to me your generation has had enormous success, and young people have come a long way in this country. Do you feel that your generation has been shut out of opportunity?

TRUSCOTT: No, I think vets have been shut out.

CAPUTO: Well, the group of us here, let's face it, is just different. Here we've got to think about the guys, Jim's guys like Snake and Bagger [characters in *Fields of Fire*]. I am not altogether sure that those guys have not been shut out or shut off from opportunities that, had they come up in another era, they would have been able to take advantage of. There does seem to be a certain amount of disenchantment, disenfranchisement, which I use in the very loose sense of the term, among them. And a kind of an almost existential attitude.

FALLOWS: I think that what's between veterans and nonveterans is the question of time lag. There's a four or five years' difference in getting started, which can be a crucial difference sometimes. I think it eventually will even out 10 years from now.

WEBB: You know, the people who were the enlisted troopers in Vietnam came from more narrow social strata than in other wars. They were younger, also. And I think you can pretty thoroughly document that for years they had major employment problems directly associated with service. Some of it intentional, some of it just by virtue of the nature of the draft. The average World War II trooper was 26 years old; he already had a profession. The average Vietnam trooper was 19; he was coming out of school. As a result, he didn't have any reemployment rights, and they did exist in World War II and they were utilized. The Vietnam guy came out of the war at a time when all this affirmative-action stuff was kicking in and he had employers reaching over his head for women and minorities in order to fill judicially sanctioned quotas, no matter what they called them.

There was a certain amount of stigma attached to his service which has, thankfully, been evaporating. But it did exist. One example. Jim, you met Mike McGarvey, who was one of my radio operators—very motivated, good Marine, lost his arm—who for years bounced around from menial job to menial job. He'd wanted to be a policeman and of course that fell by the wayside. But I and another fellow out of my platoon, one of my squad leaders who lived in Nashville, were able to finally place him in a Harley-Davidson place, at least for an interview. And the first question that I was asked by the dealer—after about five months of trying to get people just to interview him—first question I was asked by the guy was, "Look, this guy ain't a dopie, is he?" First question, right off the bat. That did exist.

CAPUTO: One important thing, and it's a negative thing that we should not do, is ever create a myth of the war being responsible for personal failures. Which has occurred. I'd like to call attention to what I think is probably the more representative experience, about those veterans who had tremendous obstacles to overcome when they came back, and overcame them. I think of one example, of one of my squad leaders who extended his tour, stayed over there, got wounded three times, lost his leg below the knee, came back to one of those gruesome VA hospitals like the one you described, where he got hooked on junk. Was on junk when he got out of the hospital. Cold-turkeyed himself. And then went on to become a high school football coach. And married a beautiful girl and raised a family and, really on his own willpower and own resources, completely patched his life together.

> **"I think we lost a generation.... I am telling you, I am dealing with thousands of people that are so disgusted and turned off that they're lost."**
> **—Robert Muller**

MULLER: I've got to tell you, I'm a little distressed by the tone of this conversation. I really am. Because I'm starting to realize how out of sync with the rest of you I think I am. I view what we're really talking about in its essence here in a much more dramatic way than I think any of you really do. From my vantage point, it's a bad situation and it's one which we have not taken serious steps to remedy.

The point is, our generation came of age with a basic willingness to serve. Two thirds of our guys in Vietnam gave of themselves willingly, voluntarily. There was no question. We do not have that same willingness on the part of people who are 18, 19, 20 years old today to render themselves to a public service, to service to the country. I go to high schools, I talk to seniors and I'm telling you, I am getting very, very troubling signs.

TRUSCOTT: I understood you, but you said you were upset about what we were saying. What's your gripe?

MULLER: My gripe is, I have a sense of a lot of people out there that is much more troubled by our experience of the past 15 years which hasn't been resolved than I think is understood here, or at least is related to here.

TRUSCOTT: Veterans? Are you talking about veterans?

MULLER: I'm talking about veterans, I'm talking about non-veterans, because when you look to what I consider the pain of Vietnam, I knew the fucking statistics. The idea of getting blown away did not stop me from going, because I fully expected to get hit. I really did. What is my pain from the Vietnam experience? I fucking believed it! I believed the American fucking dream. We're righteous. We're good. We speak for freedom.

TRUSCOTT: Bobby, we all believed it and the marvelous thing about you is you still do.

CAPUTO: I don't understand what you perceive to be the problem.

MULLER: The problem is, I think we lost a generation. I think we lost a generation of people. Our generation came of age believing. We remember. I remember with goose bumps John Kennedy's speech: "Ask not what your country can do for you, but what you can do for your country." I remember all of my classmates having been the Freedom Riders going down to the South. The civil rights movement—what could be more righteous than that? The rise of the Peace Corps. The willingness. America was something that, when I stood at the Marine Corps barracks down here in the sunset parade, I had fucking tears in my eyes as a lieutenant because I was so proud to be an American! Why did I go to Vietnam? I didn't know what the fuck was going on in Southeast Asia, but I said, "Goddamm it, the president of this country, the Congress, the leadership in this country knows a lot more about it than I do, and I fucking trust that they're doing what America stands for."

TRUSCOTT: Dammit, what's the gripe?

MULLER: Disillusionment over the leadership in this country and the fucking institutions that betrayed my fucking willingness to give my tender fucking young ass in the service of this country. And I believe what Jim said, that we were well intentioned. I don't believe we were led with malice, but our failure to recognize it once we made the error, to remedy the problem. To come back and be turned upon by the fucking politicians and the institutions and the leaders, and being called "the home front snipers," and going through the shit and being dumped on, and never being able to rehabilitate the concept of service or rehabilitate the trust and confidence in the leadership in this country is what is at the heart. I am telling you, I am dealing with thousands of people that are so disgusted and turned off that they're lost. And it's not just the veteran, it's the nonveteran as well.

CAPUTO: But what can be done about it? I think one of the problems we've got in this country is a tendency to view things apocalyptically. I don't mean to belittle the Vietnam experience, because I was the one who said that it was probably the most wrenching national experience we've had since the Civil War. But let us not forget that it was the first time that this country faced not just a major test of its foreign policy, which failed, it also had a moral challenge that it had to face that it never faced before. And it also faced what all great nations have had to face at one time or another in their history, and that is the limitations of what it can do, whether for good or ill.

Absolutely every great nation, going back to the Roman Empire, at some point has finally come up against a wall. I think about the British Empire. When it lost the American colonies in the 18th century, that was a significant and traumatic loss, not just in a material sense but in a psychological sense. The greatest military power in Europe at that time was defeated by a bunch of clowns in buckskins.

TRUSCOTT: A bunch of VC.

CAPUTO: And yet the English went on, whatever your opinions may be of the 19th-century British empire, to create a significant civilization. They went on to save Europe itself from Napoleon. They did not indulge in this recrimination, this self-flagellation, all this morbid...

WEBB: I don't share your gloom about the way that our generation is dealing with this. I'd like to give two small examples. I did two different tours on my book. I did a hardback tour in the fall of '78 and a paperback tour in the summer of '79. And in the process of doing those I did over 300 different media events, most of them radio call-in shows. And the difference in one year was phenomenal. I was lucky to get out of Boston alive in '78. I was called a murderer. I was asked if I shot heroin, the whole bit. In 1978 in Milwaukee I was doing a call-in show and a guy actually stopped the show and broke for a commercial and turned around and said, "Do you realize you're the first guy who ever came in here without first apologizing for having been in Vietnam?" That was in 1978. Yet by 1979, the mood was different. The whole attitudinal referent was different. And I think that the arts and a lot of the general literature that had come out began to move people, began to affect comprehension.

WHEELER: But different people move at different paces and I think there's a lot of grief that we put our finger on. If we did say good-bye to men we knew who were dead or if we said good-bye to part of our life or a part of our body, that grief for all sorts of reasons can take longer for some people than for others. And I think it's at least in direct proportion to the size of the wound.

MULLER: I think it's for us to call the question. We have got to promote, through public dialogue, through discussion, consideration of the very profound, complex issues that are there. Right now, our military manpower question is what is going to finally bring to a head what's been smoldering, in my opinion, under the surface about the Vietnam experience. Namely, who serves? How do you distribute that burden of service? What is the role of a citizen in this democratic country that we have?

If we learned anything out of Vietnam, we learned that the strength of a nation is a function of its will and its resolve to stand together, and until you rehabilitate the concept of service through what you perceive the Vietnam veterans to be, you're going to be hard put. You put out the call right now. You put out the call. What happens when you pass that draft registration and, let's say, 25 percent of the 19- and 20-year-olds say, "Fuck you." They stand right in front of the White House and they say, "We ain't gonna do it." What happens when a significant proportion of the population blatantly and willingly disregards the law of the land? And that's what's going to happen.

CAPUTO: I had two young kids come up to my door down at Key West who were organizing an antidraft rally. They had read my book, they interpreted the book as a pacifist book and therefore thought I would support the rally. So I sat down and said, "I can't support it because I support the draft so long as it's relatively equitable." So they said, "We'd like to hear why you do. We didn't think that somebody that wrote a book like that would." So I sat down and explained to them what my experiences had been when I was Moscow correspondent for the [Chicago] *Tribune*. What I felt our society was up against vis-à-vis the Soviet Union.

Then one of these kids said, "Well, I don't want to die for Shell Oil." And I said, "OK, that's a nice catch phrase. It looks good on a placard." I said, "What you don't realize is that you are living in the postindustrial society whose entire economy, right from the shirt you're wearing to the panty hose your girl's got on, to absolutely everything you do, is based on this particular natural resource." And I said, "What you don't realize is that the other aspects, political and social aspects, of your life are dependent on that level of economic development. You're not going to worry about freedom of speech and freedom of the press and all that sort of thing if you're living the way they do in Upper Volta." In effect, I said, what you'd be dying for is the preservation of Western industrial civilization. I said, "If you think that entire civilization isn't worth a damn in spite of all that it has achieved in the sciences, medicine, the exploration of the universe, then fine. Then don't go."

Well, it was interesting. They went ahead and they held the

rally but both of those kids—they were in the mid-20s—told me that they very much appreciated that I sat down and talked to them, that I had shown them things and said things to them that they had not realized before.

That long preamble is to the point that you will lessen—maybe you'll eliminate altogether—that kind of danger of mass civil disobedience to the law of the land when we get leaders, or even a leader, who can articulate what we are about and why. The problem that we now have is that the leaders no longer seem to articulate particularly what the dangers are that we are facing.

MULLER: Either that or we've lost the confidence that they are. We've lost the confidence that we can trust these guys.

WHEELER: The key to leadership is sacrifice and if you're saying that, then there's something wrong with our leaders.

TRUSCOTT: I think it's time we took over, man.

Cold, Stone Man

Lewis W. Bruchey

Who am I?
Child of war,
Vietnam hero,
Or America's
  whore?

Sucker'd,
This seething,
Silent soul,
"Savage beast,
A fool!"
Wasn't I
Once proud,
Once bold?

But wait.
Am I not
Like you,
From you,
You?

So I killed
Those out
To kill me.
Whose cause
Was just?
Victor or victim,
All return
To dust.

Four died
By my hand,
Viet Cong,
Hardcore.
No women,
No children,
My spoils
Of war.

Remember
The fight?
"Contact! Contact!
Slashing Talon
Seven Four!"

Remember
The blast
Of the cruel
Claymore,
Vile smell
Of death,
M-16's roar?

Remember
Young martyrs,
Grim trophies
Of war,
Innocence lost,
Baptized
In gore,
When madness
Reign'd
Cried out,
"More war!"

I do! I do!

They pin
A star
Upon my chest,
A subtle nod,
No more, no less.
Alone
I stand.
I AM THE BEST.

But wait.
Remember
The rockets,
The jungle,
The rain?

Remember
Death's grinning
  face,
Evil, masked
In pain?

Remember
Night sounds
Eyes strain'd
To see?

Remember
Death stalking
The darkness,
A reaper
To reap me?

I do! I do!

So speak softly
To me,
And do not
Stare.

Save your
  judgment,
Your sorrow,
Your pity,
Your prayer.

For I am
A cold, stone man
Of Vietnam.
Beware! Beware!

Lewis W. Bruchey was the leader of a five-man Long-Range Reconnaissance Patrol team, 75th Rangers, attached to the 1st Air Cavalry Division, from January 1970 to March 1971. Based in Phuoc Vinh, his team led the 1st Air Cavalry into Cambodia during the 1970 invasion. A veteran of 47 missions, he holds the Silver Star and the Bronze Star.

Part Three

MANY LEGACIES

INTRODUCTION

AS AMERICANS REFLECT BACK ON THE SIGNIFI-
cance of the war years, many different legacies have begun
to emerge. The essays that follow explore some of these
legacies. The authors come from varied backgrounds:

SAM BROWN was a leader of the antiwar movement as
national coordinator of the Vietnam Moratorium Committee
in 1969–70. In 1974 he was elected state treasurer of
Colorado and from 1977 to 1980 he was the director of
ACTION, the federal agency that includes the Peace Corps.

SUSAN JACOBY is a magazine writer and author of
three books, including *The Possible She*, a collection of
essays about women.

WILLIAM JAYNE was drafted in 1966 and served as a
rifleman in a Marine company. Wounded near Khe Sanh in
February 1968, he came back to graduate from the University of California, Berkeley, and now works for a trade
association in Washington.

NICHOLAS LEMANN, the youngest contributor to
this volume, is executive editor of *Texas Monthly* magazine.

TIM O'BRIEN, the novelist whose prize-winning
Going After Cacciato is excerpted in Part One of this
volume, was an Army draftee from Minnesota who served
in an infantry platoon in Vietnam.

WALLACE TERRY covered the Vietnam War for *Time*
magazine from 1967 to 1969. His documentary on black GIs
in combat, *Guess Who's Coming Home*, won an Image
award from the Hollywood NAACP. JANICE TERRY, his
wife, made 18 trips to Vietnam from her home in Singapore,
visiting every war zone.

CHAPTER NINE

Immigrants From the Combat Zone

William Jayne

WE WENT TO VIETNAM AS FRIGHTENED, LONELY young men. We came back, alone again, as immigrants to a new world. For the culture we had known dissolved while we were in Vietnam, and the culture of combat we lived in so intensely for a year made us aliens when we returned.

Most of us who fought the war as enlisted men in combat units were very young, much younger than the average enlisted man in World War II. We came to maturity just as we experienced this cultural dislocation. And we each had to do it alone.

Going there, we flew with a group of men we had known for a few weeks during training; landing, our sense of isolation increased as we were divided into replacement groups, then divided again and again until we found ourselves in platoons and assigned to squads of 10 or 12 men.

In the small-unit war of Vietnam, the platoon of 25 to 30 was the largest unit in which men could expect to build friendships based on shared experience—the tension of living continuously under the threat of combat. The platoon seldom left the combat zone. When we went on R and R, we went alone. Finally, we trickled home alone, pulled out of combat on dates based on our day of arrival and again grouped with strangers for the trip home.

On a packed 707 flying home from Okinawa, I found one man I had gone through boot camp with. Just one man out of 60 or so who had gone to Vietnam immediately after advanced infantry training. Dave and I each knew eight or 10 members of that recruit platoon who had been killed or had been wounded seriously enough to be transferred out. We each knew a few others who had made it through their tours of duty and gone home ahead of us. What had become of all the others? We didn't know, but it served to heighten our sense of being alone.

Being cut off from our units, our clans, was perhaps even more dispiriting. We could scarcely avoid feeling that we had abandoned our brothers. Riding the bus in from El Toro Marine Corps Air Station to the Los Angeles airport, along with civilians who studiously avoided noticing our uniforms, watching the business of the city unfold, we knew all the time that men we had lived with constantly for months were still wet, tired, hungry, perhaps even dead or wounded, 8,000 miles away across that ocean.

We had been processed through El Toro as perfunctorily and impersonally as we had filtered through Da Nang 13 months earlier on our way to our units. We stood in line to get our orders stamped and receive checks for back pay, and that was it.

Dave and I took the same flight to New York, adding three more time zones to the eight we had crossed between Vietnam and California. Like travelers in a time machine, we didn't even know what day it was. The landscape we saw around the airports was as strange to us as if recalled from a dream; ordinary things like street signs, paved roads, traffic lights and the variety of clothes people wore seemed wonderful.

We landed at JFK and Dave was heading for La Guardia to catch a plane home, so we shared a cab between airports. Sal, our cab driver, had been a Marine in World War II. He stopped at a bar in Queens and called on the patrons to stand us a round of drinks. There were no takers. We bought and drank a few beers and went on.

At La Guardia, Dave and I parted. I've never heard from him or tried to contact him since. Sal took me to the Port Authority bus terminal, where I waited through the night for a bus to my hometown in the Hudson Valley.

I had grown up with deep roots in that small town, steeped in a tradition of service to country. Members of my father's family served in every major war fought by the United States. My father

and his three brothers all served in World War II, three of them in
heavy combat.

That town now seemed alien and somehow destructive,
threatening. In Vietnam, I had served the last six months of my
tour as a rifleman in a Marine company that saw first little and
then heavy combat around Khe Sanh during the Tet Offensive of
1968. I had developed skills and personality traits that protected
me both physically and mentally while in Vietnam: patience, an
informed sense of night vision, doggedness, humorous bravado
and cynicism. Orders were to be received with meaningless
derision; institutions were to be mistrusted; difficulties were to be
surmounted with camouflaged persistence. In upstate New York,
those skills and traits were seldom noticed and never admired for
what they were—professional expertise.

I served my remaining six months in the Marine Corps and
quickly migrated to California, where I soon formed friendships
with three fellow immigrants, recently returned Vietnam veterans
who, like me, did not know what to do with the excess psychic
baggage of Vietnam experience in a culture that did not value or
even recognize the existence of that experience.

Like all combat veterans, we could not help but agree with
Hemingway that "Abstract words such as glory, honor, courage,
or hallow were obscene beside the concrete names of villages, the
numbers of roads, the names of rivers, the numbers of regiments
and the dates." William Manchester, in his memoir, *Goodbye,
Darkness,* notes that, for the Marine combat veteran of World War
II, those concrete names had been "Buna and Suribachi; the
Kokoda Trail and Tarawa, the First Marine Division and the
Eleventh Airborne; the Kumusi and the Asa Kawa; December 7,
1941, and V-J Day."

We had such concrete names imbedded in our psyches, too.
Names like Con Thien and the Arizona Territory; the Rockpile
and Hill 881; the 9th Marines and the 5th Marines. Unlike
Manchester's, however, those concrete terms meant nothing in the
new world of America in the '70s. The concrete names of World

War II, the Marines' heroic quest across the Pacific, are a part of our national mythology. No one knows that over 6,000 Marines died in Quang Nam province in the course of the Vietnam War.

We could agree with Hemingway and Manchester that glorious abstractions were obscene alongside the concrete names but, unlike them, our memories were dominated by the feeling that those concrete names—and all they represented—were useless. Our combat experience, the seminal event in our lives, was not viewed in the context of being right, wrong, glorious or respectful. It was simply useless.

The experience, then, was closeted away. For 10 years the memories would flit across one's consciousness at inappropriate times: a pause in idle conversation around a swimming pool; suddenly, inexplicably, the mind recalling some strangely named place like Khe Sanh, the introspective pause evaporating and then the mind returning, somewhat absently, to the idle conversation.

For the four of us, fellow immigrants going to college in California, the memories of concrete names, the combat skills and traits were like the ability to speak Polish or to understand Italian body-language gestures.

Our "homeland" was the surreal jungle of Vietnam, where everyone was an enemy. We talked through the late nights of growing up in the jungle—our individual brushes with deadly enemies—and our impressions of this new world we wanted to be a part of.

We had learned in that jungle that self-preservation is the imperative that drives all humanity, and we had concrete knowledge that institutions are often the gravest threat to self-preservation. Intuitively, we avoided contact with institutions and relied on our own individual strengths to find a niche in the new world.

One of my friends took his degree in American studies and became a postman. Another is a PhD candidate at the University of California but works as a movie projectionist, refusing to write his doctoral dissertation. Both have become leaders in their union locals, despite their eccentric values. Somehow our society still views combat experience as a test of leadership.

But it is still an open question whether Vietnam combat veterans like my projectionist friend Chuck will work within the system to become leaders on a larger scale. Leadership is not consistent with rootlessness and distrust of institutions.

With our "old country" values and memories locked away within us, Vietnam veterans have often, like Chuck, allowed themselves to be assimilated, to a degree, within the larger culture. We allow others to see within us what they want to see, as long as it is not threatening to us. Yet we often work to frustrate the expectations that large institutions, like the University of California, may have for us.

We have built bunkers that protect us from forces that threaten the sense of individual integrity we forged within ourselves as we grew up in the combat culture of Vietnam.

For those of us whose bunkers weren't strong enough, whose sense of integrity was not well founded, there have been further casualties of that war. It is well documented that Vietnam veterans have experienced higher rates of divorce, alcoholism, drug addiction and suicide than others of our generation, and it is likely that those statistics are highest in the ranks of combat veterans.

The majority of us, however, have found our places somewhere within American society, while retaining a sense of being separate from the rest of our generation. The alienation of the combat experience—the sense of guilt, loss and betrayal—has been heightened by our feeling of how irrelevant it is. Still, like other generations of immigrants, we are making our contributions to society, if only as a by-product of the drive to protect our own integrity.

CHAPTER TEN

The War and Race

Wallace and Janice Terry

THEY SHARED THE SAME MUD. THEY SPILLED THE same blood. Black and white soldiers soldiering together. In the annals of American military history, a new chapter was about to be written. For during the first three years of the Vietnam War, the military seemed to represent the most integrated institution in American society. For the first time blacks were fully integrated in combat and fruitfully employed in positions of leadership. In the swamps of the Mekong Delta, in search-and-destroy missions across the rubber plantations to the rolling hills of the Central Highlands, in the set-piece battles of the DMZ, on the swift boats and off the carrier decks of the 7th Fleet, in the cockpits of helicopters and fighter jets above both Vietnams, as frogman or doctor, as sniper or engineer, as machine gunner or chaplain, the black soldier won a badge of valor he expected his nation to honor forever. "I've fought in three wars and three more wouldn't be too many to defend my country," Daniel "Chappie" James Jr., a black Air Force colonel stationed at Ubon, Thailand, said in 1967. "I love America and as she has weaknesses or ills, I'll hold her hand."

Eleven percent of the American population, blacks always died in Vietnam at a greater rate. In 1965 and 1966, blacks were 23 percent of those Americans killed in action. Where blacks were a third of the crack brigade of the 101st Airborne and half of its reconnaissance commanders, the front lines became known as "Soulville." In 1967, blacks were 20 percent of the combat forces, 25 percent of the elite troops, and up to 45 percent of the airborne rifle platoons; 20 percent of the Army fatalities were black, 11 percent of the Marine. By 1968, the war's peak year, 14 percent of the U.S. combat deaths were black.

Despite the high casualties, there was little to support the charges of some black leaders that black soldiers were being unwillingly used as "cannon fodder." Most black soldiers, in 1966 and 1967, were anxious to prove themselves in combat and agreed that the war was worth fighting to halt the spread of communism. Because past discrimination deprived them of full opportunity, fewer blacks than whites possessed the preparation and training for entrance into more highly skilled occupations such as electronics, and thus they ended up carrying guns or pushing brooms.

Newspapers, magazines and television networks back home heralded most the spirit of brotherhood between blacks and whites in the foxhole. Near Bien Hoa, for instance, Specialist 5 Cleophas Mims, a black medic for the 1st Infantry Division, dragged a wounded tank commander to the back deck of his tank, covered his body with his own as a rubber tree cut apart by communist fire crashed down upon them. The commander was white. Blacks saving whites, whites saving blacks—it all became commonplace in this war.

But there was another side to the story, a side that was obscured during the first years in Vietnam. Later, as the war ground on, the other side became more important, more visible, more significant for the future.

Brotherhood at the front lines was one thing. But back at the bases, the signs of future trouble were more obvious. Beneath the integrated surface of the war, the old prejudices still festered. Confederate flags flew from barracks and trucks. On the walls of bars and latrines were scrawled such graffiti as "niggers eat shit" and "I'd prefer a gook to a nigger." The black soldier still found himself doing more than his share of the dirty work. Promotions, awards and coveted rear-area assignments were too often slow in coming the black soldier's way, however well he fought or however high the proportion of his front-line casualties. There were, at the end of 1967, only two black generals among 1,346 generals and admirals, one in the Army and one in the Air Force.

The Marines had no colonels. And across the battlefield only two battalion commanders in 380 were black.

Meanwhile a new black soldier appeared, born of the American failure in the war against black poverty and white racism, but born most of all of the new black spirit that sprang from the ruins of Harlem and Watts, from the fallen manhood of Malcolm X and from the blood of Martin Luther King.

Unify, the brothers said. Show your brother—your blood— where he can come for strength, protection and understanding. Show the Man with his foot on your neck. Show the Chuck. The Rabbit. The Devil. The Beast. The Swine.

So when Blood met Blood, clenched fists were raised. At meeting points like the Soul Kitchen on Saigon's outskirts, Blood greeted Blood over spareribs, grits, corn bread and chitlins in endless Black Power handshakes and grips that ended with Blood giving Blood knowledge by tapping him on the head, or Blood vowing to die for Blood by crossing the chest, Roman Legion-style. The Bloods of each division, of each battalion and of each company would have their own special way of giving up power, of laying down the dap, of gripping and greeting the hand of the brother Blood.

In increasing numbers, the Blood, even along the borders of Cambodia and Laos, organized to protest discrimination in punishment, promotion and assignment. Some chose to live by themselves, asking whites to leave or driving them from hootches they shared. There were some, like the Bloods of a company of 1st Cavalry Division attack troops, who startled white commanders by entering battle in black battle dress: black berets, black shirts, black beads and black gloves. From late 1967 racial insults swept the battle zones, leading to fights and riots. Injuries often followed, and some were killed. The various commands were forced to establish race-relations committees, but conditions were not fully ameliorated until many alleged black troublemakers were discharged, often arbitrarily, and the last Americans were removed from Vietnam.

It became clearer, however, that the black soldier would forevermore be respected not only by the enemies of his uniform but by his white comrades-in-arms—even those who wore Ku Klux Klan costumes, burned crosses and waved Confederate flags on the fields of Vietnam. As a black soldier in the 9th Infantry Division explained the change during a pause in a firefight near Dong Tam: "Nobody ever calls me nigger when I'm carrying my grenade launcher."

Once home, black veterans faced severe employment problems. Many had been unfairly given less-than-honorable discharges. In a study conducted by the Center for Policy Research in New York in 1977, 28 percent of the black veterans surveyed were unemployed but only 3 percent of the white veterans were. Black veterans also found that the antiwar movement had drained white support from some civil rights organizations. And the most militant black organizations were suppressed or destroyed by federal and local police action. The Great Society programs disappeared under Richard Nixon, and the Supreme Court upheld Bakke, dealing a blow to affirmative action. The thoughts of the nation turned to the rights of women at home and the freedom of hostages in Iran. And so, as the 1980s began, most black veterans remained a despairing population, whose sacrifice was still unrecognized and unrewarded but whose anger had yet to launch them into guerrilla warfare against the walls of injustice.

A few days after the inauguration of Ronald Reagan as the 40th president of the United States, we invited several members of the black community to share their thoughts and memories of the war and its aftermath with two black veterans. One of the veterans had been a Marine grunt, the other a helicopter machine gunner. Although one was an accomplished artist and the other was a seasoned photographer, each was having trouble finding enough work to survive. Here are some of the things they had to say:

MALIK EDWARDS: I'm from New Orleans. Plaquemines Parish. Out in the country. I was like the first person in my family to finish high school. I was 17. There was nothing for you to do. My parents couldn't afford to send me to college. I wasn't big enough to work. But the Marine Corps took me. It was like, the Marine Corps builds men. And I wanted to be a man.

I went to Vietnam in 1965 with the original 1st Battalion, 9th Marines. If you were black, the only way you got out of the infantry was if you had some really hellfire IQ. The first night every Marine battalion landed in Vietnam, a black was killed. So they made up for the fact that we didn't die enough in World War I, World War II or Korea. We definitely made up for it in Vietnam.

They called me a shitbird because I stayed in trouble. Nobody could control me, so they made me the point. That means I'd be the first one out there. Well, after a while you develop a way of handling this. You say, "I'd rather be first, because if anybody's going to be in charge of my life, I want it to be me." You learned that the point usually survived. It was the people behind you that got killed. Every time you turned around, your brothers were getting killed. It seemed like if they didn't like you, they set you up on enough patrols that you either got wounded or killed.

They used to tell us stuff like, "If they're in black, they're the enemy." The South Vietnamese Army trained in a black uniform. So as far as we were concerned, they were enemy. So our whole thing was kill, kill, kill—even killing South Vietnamese soldiers by mistake.

I didn't have no conscience about politics. I knew that there was racism, but I figured if we fought hard enough that we would be accepted somewhere along the line. But I started finding out that it didn't make no difference. No matter how many of us fought or how many of us died.

When I came back from Vietnam, I got married. I got it

together and made sergeant. Then I started reading books about black history. It was the first time I had a view of my history and what had been done to us. I knew about slavery, but merely a hint of Nat Turner. Then all of a sudden, Africa became real to me. And Tarzan was jive. Then I became angry because I was in the Marine Corps and the Marine Corps had always been used against Third World people. So then I wanted to join the Movement. So I started protesting. As a Marine Corps sergeant? Unh, unh, buddy. So obviously, I landed in jail. And I got kicked out of the Corps after six years, eight months and eight days.

First, I tried to get a job. But because I had a BCD, nothing was happening for me. Even blacks wouldn't hire me, because I was one of them young militants wearing all that black stuff. So one day I walked into the Black Panther Party office. It just blew my mind. The independence. The fact that there was no fear of the police. Talking about self-determination. Trying to make Malcolm's message real. So I joined.

Most of the real Panthers were Vietnam veterans. Policemen were afraid of us. This was the first time that black people had stood up to the state since Nat Turner. I mean armed. Ready to go down. For real. But we really didn't understand what was happening. We didn't understand the times. We couldn't really capitalize. All we wanted was to kick whitey's ass. We didn't think about buying property, looking for some economic independence. We were just out there showing off.

Well, obviously that began to play out because the power structure started building up the Jesse Jacksons and putting money into the poverty programs. Nobody wanted to follow the Panthers when they could go down to the poverty program and get a check and act like they were going to school. Then Agnew came out and said, "Hey, don't you even mention them." That wiped us out of the media. Just like the media had given us rise, the media brought us down. And then the FBI stepped up their program of harassment of our supporters. The reality of life, of money, of politics, just started to take its toll. And everybody started to go back home. Back to the real world.

Now I'm 35. And an artist drawing unemployment.

DICK GREGORY: From 1954 to 1956 I served in the Army as a private. In New York, in California, at the Pentagon. All over. Back in those days and during World War II, we used to say that going into the Army was decent. It meant getting the GI bill, going to school, maybe being a lawyer or a doctor one day. You could get your teeth fixed. Three meals. Get married, too, because you will have an allotment. It was not a patriotic thing for black folks so much as an escape route to participate into the things of a greedy society which totally passed us by.

We looked at war then as nothing but glorious. When society said to our grandmas, "Thou shall not kill," it did not mean war. We thought the military would make Billy behave. If Billy died in Bataan, we would say, "He was a fine boy. 19. I got his last letter." In my neighborhood, few blacks died young that we weren't ashamed to talk about. These white folks gave us a chance to die. In death, they accepted me more. We wanted nothing more than a flag-draped casket.

Vietnam gave me a conscience. It was the first war where a segment of white folks I respected—Harvard and Yale—said the war was wrong. And you couldn't call Muhammad Ali a long-haired faggot or hippie. He was our hero. He was us. He didn't go to Harvard or Howard. When they stripped him of the chance to earn a living because he refused to fight, he became all of us After all, he was everything—strong, yellow, good-looking, even grandmas liked him.

So I marched on the Pentagon. I stopped eating solid food and I swore I wouldn't shave again until we got out of Southeast Asia.

Today I look at the military as welfare. And I look at the draft not as drafting, but giving you a chance to be killed. And I would consider myself a failure as a father and as a human if any of the children my wife and I produced would kill anyone under any circumstances. I've programmed them not to run from the draft, not to resist it, but to be willing to take whatever the penalty is to refuse it

CARLOS CAMPBELL: I played football at Michigan State. Back then, like Greg says, there was no thought about not going into the military. For me, the choice was either going into the Marine Corps or going into the Navy. My girlfriend said she liked the Navy uniform, so I said I'd go Navy. The funny part is she ended up marrying my roommate, a Marine.

The Navy taught me to fly. It was like playing football. At State there was a pregame ritual of just sort of strutting. Going around with these helmets. Just sort of walking around, you know, getting ready to kick somebody's ass. And before you go on the field, you know people would see you as a warrior. The same thing is true in the military. You put on that flight suit, man, and it's like you're getting a whole new body. You're getting rid of those 15 pounds you don't need. You put on that anti-G suit. Then all of a sudden, take your .38 and you slip it up here and you get your bullets and your tracer bullets sliding across your chest. Get your little life vest coming down here. Get this great big, beautiful helmet going to protect you, right. Get your great big flight boots. And all this shit. Step out to that airplane, and you might as well be getting into bed with Denise Nicholas or Pam Grier. Because you just go *Oooooo*. You just gotta get it off now. You are in the preorgasmic mindset of the military person. And when you're in the airplane, and you fire a rocket, and you hear that whoosh leave your wing, then all of a sudden it hits. POW. It's like an orgasm.

In the early '60s I flew patrols off the coast of China, North Korea and the Soviet Union. When I came back to the States in '64, I was assigned to the Defense Intelligence Agency at the Pentagon. When the war got hot, I began to feel kind of guilty because like, hey, I'm not over there. I wanted to be with a fighter squadron or an attack squadron so I could fire rockets or missiles or drop bombs. That's where my head was.

When it really started getting close was when Joe Henriquez got it. Joe was Navy. On his first flight off the carrier, he got jumped over the North. He called in for air cover and got cleaned up. Then he went downtown Hanoi to keep from getting shot down, because obviously, the Migs would not shoot him down right on top of Hanoi. So he just went downtown Hanoi. This is a bad motherfucker. A couple of fighters took care of the guys on top of him, so he goes over to Haiphong and knocks out two or three patrol boats. But later he got what we call a cold cock shot, an underpower shot off the carrier. It killed him. They gave Joe full military honors at Arlington Cemetery. His wife, Carole, was about eight months pregnant. His two children were there, too. And Joe was buried, and Carole received the flag over her big belly. We were not in any kind of military formation, so when it was over these two gravediggers came over. One of them said to me, "Hey, man. Hey, man. Was he black? Was he black?" I said, "Yes. He was Lt. Cmdr. Henriquez." And the other grave man turned around and said, "See, man? I told you. I told you they buried brothers with military honors." It was 1966. And I was thinking of the hypocrisy of democracy. Carole would walk out of that cemetery and it would be business as usual.

CHARLES COBB: I spent my formative years in Washington, D.C., and at Classical High School in Springfield, Mass. By the time I came out of high school, what really affected me was the student sit-ins. I mean you saw the students from Nashville doing something. They were being aggressive. So I made the decision to go to Mississippi. That totally obliterated any thoughts about joining the Army like some of my friends. I went down to Mississippi at the end of '61 and stayed to '67. I was a field secretary for SNICK, the Student Nonviolent Coordinating Committee. I didn't even bother to register for the draft. When the card came, I sent it to Oregon. The thing to do was to send it to the farthest post office that you could think of. There was some concern in the Movement about so many of us being draft age. But like there was a tacit understanding reached between us in Mississippi and Bobby Kennedy that if we were doing this voter-registration organizing, then the draft thing would just be ignored. It would be deferred.

In '61, '62 and '63 you just weren't thinking about the military, the Vietnamese, the Cambodians or anybody. In Mississippi there was a lot of violence. People were getting killed and houses were being blown up. All of our conversation was in terms of the Klan, the Association for the Preservation of the White Race, and getting black people to move. Then the Atlantic City thing happened with the Mississippi Freedom Democratic Party protest at the [1964] Democratic National Convention. We discovered that liberal America wasn't prepared to deal with black people. We felt sold out, not by the right wing of the Democratic Party, but by that part run by Hubert Humphrey, Joe Rauh and particularly Walter Reuther. They arm-twisted Martin King. That was when we began to question everything about the country. We had convinced people to risk their lives to register to vote. We'd tell people, "If you don't like it, the way to change things would be to get political power." But when it came to the crunch, we saw that the good guys put our interests last and put their interests first.

Then Sammy Younge was murdered in Alabama. He went to college at Tuskegee, joined the Navy, and then worked with us. He wanted to use a toilet at a gas station. This was after the '64 Civil Rights Act. The station owner killed him for using the so-called white toilet. Shot him. He bled to death there at the gas station. Vietnam was beginning to get a little visibility in the media. So we were even angrier because Sammy had been a sailor.

But the specific incident which made us sharply conscious of Vietnam was in '65. There was a picture in a news magazine showing a Vietnamese on the ground. A U.S. soldier had a bayonet stuck in him. Our reaction was that this was a white guy messing with a colored guy. The next year we wrote the SNICK anti-Vietnam War statement which resulted immediately in the refusal of the Georgia state legislature to seat Julian Bond. We came to the conclusion that there was something fundamentally flawed with the system here in the United States, which led to the war as well as to racial oppression in the South.

CAROLYN PAYTON: I'm from Norfolk, Virginia. Came to Howard University in 1959 as a psychologist. Was captivated by John Kennedy and his "ask not" speech. So I joined the Peace Corps in 1964. Went to the Caribbean in 1967 and stayed there until 1970. The war impacted on me as a Peace Corps country director in light of the changes in the nature of the volunteers we got in the field. In the early '60s the people who joined were pretty much idealistic, dedicated young Americans who thought that they could truly help Third World people. Toward the later '60s we were getting the drug people and the Vietnam draft dodger. Like in your movement, it was a tacit understanding that if you served in the Peace Corps you could avoid going to Vietnam. I was very, very concerned about the level of people we were getting, especially whites who were patronizing or unconcerned and insensitive to the needs of Third World people. Another problem that we had was that many young people we recruited wanted to use their position in Third World countries to speak out against Vietnam and embarrass the host nations. The most widely publicized incident of this type was when an American in Chile wrote a letter back to *The New York Times* as a Peace Corps volunteer opposing the Vietnam War.

I can remember coming home and being amazed at the body count on television. I could not believe Americans had become so callous. Walter Cronkite would give that score just as if it were for a football game. Americans sat passively through their dinner. It just blew my mind.

You must recognize from the gray hair that World War II was my war. And even then, one could not help but recognize that the decision to drop the atom bomb was not made for Europe but for Japan. So I've always been very conscious of the fact that

Vietnam was a war of white against "gooks." I've always been concerned that somehow we as blacks must recognize that we're fighting our own color and our own kind. I'm very, very aware of the fact that when the deal goes down, it is always going to be the whites against the nonwhites. I will bet you money, if any of you are around at the time, that even Russia is going to be accepted before the South African black. America will join forces with those "hated" Russians before they will join forces with people of color.

Finally, I would say that I saw something very positive as a result of the Vietnam War. For the first time that we've had armed forces, the American black was indeed allowed a position of equality and full responsibility. Malik sort of sarcastically said that the Marines promised to make a man of him. But, sweetie, you did get some experience being a Marine that made you different than you would have been had you stayed down in Louisiana.

EDWARDS: Oh, I don't doubt that for one second.

PAYTON: And I also believe that you learned to be responsible for yourself, and know what it means to have power. You never forget that. And I think a lot of the black Vietnam veterans who came back did not simply go back to the hills and pick up that hoe and climb behind that mule, because Vietnam gave them a chance to experience power. And it cost. A hell of a lot, but I think we are a different group of people as a result of that experience.

STEVE HOWARD: I was brought up by one parent, my mother. She was a maid at George Washington Hospital here in D.C. She always tried to instill in us that we had to get out and get it the best way we could. As long as we didn't steal it or break the rules. That led me to college. But I was not exempt from The Big Snatch. I got drafted in '66. I went to Vietnam on Christmas Day, 1966. I was in combat aviation, a helicopter battalion in the Army. Helicopters that I flew could launch so much destruction, launch about 52 missiles and about 20,000 rounds of ammunition. Just like little bomber bees. You know how hornets are when they are around you? They're like hornets. But with all that firepower.

I just want to tell you a little thing about a helicopter company: It does nothing but destroy. I was a machine gunner. I did the same thing every day. I got up in the morning at 6, smoked a joint, went to mess, went to the flight line, and went on and did what I had to do. And every time that I would get shot down, I ended up in either Cam Ranh Bay or Vung Tau. In Vung Tau, you had the American hospital here and you had the Viet Cong hospital over there. And nobody ever fired on Vung Tau. At all. Vung Tau was like it wasn't in the war. And Cam Ranh was the same. The only thing they put up was the shark net on the beach to keep people from being eaten up.

Then I started taking heroic pictures of my colonel. So he took me out of combat. He didn't like to hang out there with the heavy doers. He'd just go out after the firefight was over and fly around and say, "Well, we wiped out all of this." Then he'd go back. I figured he wasn't looking to die, and I didn't want to be anywhere with anybody who didn't care as much as he cared about living. So I was now a combat photographer.

The last time I got wounded, they sent me home. I became a spy, as the saying goes. I won't say intelligence. I used to go out to Kent State, different universities, or whatever, and photograph people for the Pentagon. To document how the yahoos was acting up. Now I'm a photographer. I free-lance. I prostitute my skills to whomever can afford the price.

EDWARDS: We're the most educated group of soldiers that ever went to war. We went to war believing in more freedoms than anybody who had gone to war before us. So when we got to Vietnam, we were just too intelligent to go for that madness. Immediately we realized that we were not heroes.

I remember when I killed a person for the first time. He ran up on me, and I took him out. That was the first time that I realized that the Vietnamese was a human being. All of a sudden my religious upbringing came to play. Thou shalt not kill! I sat down and started freaking out. This sergeant came over and said, "That was beautiful, man. That was fucking beautiful. This is fucking beautiful." This man, his guts is out, and he had this sound that was just freaking me out. So I said, "Let me put him out of his misery." The sergeant kept on yapping, kept on glorifying. And I couldn't stand it. So I just shot the man in the head. Right past the sergeant. I had to finish killing him.

And then, on top of that, they made me drag the body back. Now, I'm really freaking. Nobody said, "Are you all right?" Then the body started to smell.

PAYTON: So that was the body count.

EDWARDS: Right. Right. So I'm dragging this guy back, and his arm falls off. I gotta pick his arm up, 'cause you got to bring all of him back to this . . . this hero's welcome. "Ed. Killer Ed." Everybody's running around tripping, calling me Killer Ed, Killer Ed. I gotta act like I'm cool, but I am freaking out.

Here's another thing what happened. Now check how my shit works. It was a bamboo snake, right? I blew his head off. Then this old man started running. The sergeant said, "Get him, Edwards." I missed the old man, but I had just hit this little snake. So the sergeant said, "Goddam, Edwards. Get 'im, Brooks." Brooks fired. Round goes in window. Catches the old man as he turns the corner. He was going to warn these kids in this schoolroom that the Marines were coming. So Brooks ends up murdering all those children. He freaks out. Now we're really tripping. But how can you come back home and tell people that?

GREGORY: In World War II, a brother could come back home to a tavern and brag. It was like sex then, too, being a hero. But black women knew that in Vietnam, women and children got killed. Villages were destroyed. So we couldn't talk our boasts on the corner. We couldn't come back to the arms of our ladies as heroes. And it was the only war where the old folks found out we were on drugs. We all knew boys got drunk and got women in war. But not drugs.

EDWARDS: I came back home telling lies. About Vietnam. I was a hero and what a great war it was, and how wonderful it was doing all those things. Really. What I was telling was a story of World War II. I made my lies up to fit the psyche of World War II. But in my gut, I was dying. And it wasn't until after I got out of the Panther Party that I faced the reality of what I had experienced. I was fantasizing. The Black Panther Party was a fantasy. I was so broken down and just so depressed.

GREGORY: If you had died in the jungle, the VC would have buried you and the white boy in a common grave. But if your two bodies had been shipped back to the U.S., you couldn't be buried in the same cemetery in many cities. That's a sad commentary when you are treated better by an enemy than a friend at home.

HOWARD: Vietnam comes back to me every day. Sometimes I fall totally out of sync with what's going on around me. I figure if I'm educated, and I know what to do, then why am I falling apart? I'm not drugging out every day. I'm not psyching myself out every day. I think the war is coming back to haunt us. Some people, it takes 15 or 20 years for it to come back. And we have lost the unity of black GIs over there, because over here the stress is too much. It's hard as the dickens to sit down and explain to my mother, too, how emotionally messed up I am because she worked all her life to make me strong. Now, in 1981, it is a job just to hold myself together. When I think about all that destruction I dropped on people. They still running around. Because the stuff we dropped was white phosphorus— "Willie Peter." It don't stop burning. This was totally out of my way of living. There was no way that I was supposed to have gone through this.

COBB: What troubles me is that the so-called American defeat is not attributed to the strength of the Vietnamese. To the organization of the Vietnamese. To the will of the Vietnamese. Not to anything internal to Vietnam. People talk about the war. But they say America lost its will, or never had its will, or Congress tied our hands.

HOWARD: But what are we going to do about the children? What are we going to teach them? What are we going to do about kids who play the video games?

EDWARDS: I see you're falling into that same trick bag we always get caught up in.

HOWARD: Let me finish. The 7-Eleven stores now have game machines. Let me tell you why they have the game machines. They have the game machines because they get the kids that got the quarters that they will be spending for their lunch, for their nutrition.

EDWARDS: Spending lunch money for their nutrition? Come on, man.

HOWARD: The kids come in there in their Calvin Kleins. They're shooting space invaders. They're shooting rockets. They're shooting tanks. And all they worry about is getting their initials on those game machines. That's all little brothers and sisters are thinking about. Getting their initials for the best score. Do you get my point?

EDWARDS: Well, I don't need to eat the whole pie to see what it tastes like.

HOWARD: We got to teach the children. Do you get my point, Blood?

EDWARDS: Steve, what are you talking about?

HOWARD: Don't you see? There's war in those game machines.

CHAPTER ELEVEN

The Legacy of Choices

Sam Brown

COUNCIL BLUFFS, IOWA, WAS HOME TO ME. I WAS born there, went to school there, built hot rods there, and was for three years the outstanding ROTC cadet while in high school there. When I was growing up it never occurred to me that America could be wrong. The pattern of my upbringing and the texture of my day-to-day existence were solidly Midwestern and Republican; Dad belonged to the Rotary and everyone in the family went to church on Sunday. The world was an orderly, tidy place, and my place in it was secure. Even John Kennedy's death didn't upset that world. After all, his death was the act of a madman, not the result of structural defects in the American system. But other signs of the times began to erode my orderly world.

I was in college in Redlands, Calif., in 1962 when students began to question why the state imposed a ban on communist speakers. This struck me as a peculiar way to define a "free" society. I didn't see how it fit with what I had been taught in high school civics back in Abraham Lincoln High School, and it surely didn't fit my budding libertarian conservative political philosophy. This occurred about the same time as the Free Speech Movement was developing at Berkeley and the first Freedom Riders were taking buses through the South. The result was that I began to question everything I had believed about America. I questioned why the migrants who passed through Redlands lived the way they did. I questioned why the University officials at Redlands and Berkeley and the state officials in Sacramento were so virulent in their defense of order but unwilling to defend the First Amendment. Then came the fall of the Diem government, the initial U.S. combat presence in Vietnam and the U.S. intervention in the Dominican Republic. At that point, I was sure that everything the U.S. government supported abroad was wrong. By the time of the escalation of the war I knew without any very fundamental analysis of the facts that the war had to be stopped merely because it was our war. By 1969 my views would be codified in articles, essays and public debate, but in 1965 my thoughts were more visceral than intellectual.

For me it was an exciting time. Those of us who opposed the war all seemed to be young, wear our hair long, and at least some of my friends believed that legalizing marijuana and popularizing rock and roll were of the same degree of importance as ending the war in Vietnam. The press said we were doing exciting things (even the nearly universal editorial support for the war only convinced us that our work was important). Suddenly there were no unquestioned truths. Skepticism was the only acceptable intellectual posture, cynicism was almost always rewarded by an accommodating reality and paranoia, which seemed only trendy in 1967, turned out to be justified by 1973. Often after leaving the office of one or another of the antiwar organizations at midnight or 1 or 2 in the morning, we would continue our debate over Marcuse or Norman O. Brown or Marx or Freud for several more hours. They were heady times with a facade of sacrifice (long hours, little pay, a certain approbation among our elders) but with a taste of responsibility and seriousness far beyond our years.

It was not a time when people were particularly tolerant of each other. We were young, smart, intellectual (so we thought) and committed to a moral cause. We believed ourselves patriots defending America's ideals. They (and by that time "they" were almost always older) were, as far as we were concerned, narrow-minded, intolerant and unwilling to respect our patriotism. It was a time of intense certainty. The ideas espoused by either group were almost automatically opposed by the other. Each side held to its half-thoughts and unfounded assumptions. Each side hurt the other. My father and I grew apart even though he respected the seriousness of my intentions and endured late-night telephone threats and shunning from his fellow "Christian" churchgoers because of my activities.

I had little time to absorb the emotional impact of these events, but I knew that the orderly, tidy world of my Midwest past was not mine. I was on the outside. I wanted the political, economic and institutional status quo to be changed and that change had to come quickly. I distrusted big business and the big military and was skeptical about the capacity of the federal government to ensure both a measure of economic equity and civil liberties.

I also believed that with the right people, the political will and a few hundred thousand dollars, national policy could be changed for the better. I assumed that my generation, and specifically those of us who shared such a commitment to America in our efforts to end the war, could be a powerful influence for the better. With such certainty I began my public life.

Now, almost ten years later, my certainty has been tempered by events and experience. I have learned some lessons, one of which is plainly evident: My generation has not saved the world, nor has it yet changed the political topography of this nation. But the war that was so much part of our growing up continues to have an impact on our society and on how we shape our personal lives.

Even my way of thinking has been influenced by the war. The very structure and direction of the antiwar movement required a sense of direct response to events and an ordered process of getting there. Petitions had to be signed, candidates found to run for public office and demonstrations mounted to urge the end of the war. Things had to be done. In a way, the very organization of the antiwar movement was ironically similar to that of the military. The long-term consequences were also sometimes as mindlessly destructive as those of the war. Those on the fringe of the resistance to the war took up violence as an answer.

And, like the military, those who actively dissented developed a sense of camaraderie that grew from shared risks, values and experiences. If our reunions were never quite so structured as those at West Point, our identities have still been reaffirmed more than once by reminders of what we were doing during the war, the shared history has been used as a touchstone for future relations. The war became part of one's resumé.

The tag line "antiwar leader" has been as much a part of my name as an MD is of any doctor's. The tag line has been both something to be proud of and yet, at the same time, a very personal and sad reminder that the country was still divided. Memories have lingered.

I was not surprised, then, that when I was named the director of ACTION in 1976 my activities were closely scrutinized by some members of Congress. Even though I had spent two years being the state treasurer of Colorado, paying my dues, so to speak, I was typed by those who did not know me as the "radical 33-year-old," a phrase I once thought was a contradiction in terms.

President Carter's decision to swear me and Max Cleland, the Vietnam War amputee who became the head of the Veterans Administration, in on the same day seemed to signify a new tolerance, a willingness to find common ground for those of our generation who had been split apart by the decisions of another generation. But for a significant number of conservatives and indeed for some people on the left, my going to Washington to run ACTION did not change the context of how I was perceived. For those on the far right, I was suspect, the radical who was subverting the federal government from within. For those on the left, my commitment to the general principles which we had struggled to uphold had to be tested: Was I still one of them? Would I sell out?

After so many years of being on the outside, of being part of a political culture that was skeptical even of itself and often looked at the world in a "them" versus "us" dichotomy, being in public office was like stepping into a different culture with different customs, mannerisms, expectations, language and people. I felt comfortable and perfectly capable of being part of this culture, given my background and education, but my allegiance was split.

Intellectually, I remained rooted in the skepticism and out-rage that had defined so much of my thinking. I looked for advice and counsel to the network of people who came to Washington at the same time as I did and had belonged to the antiwar movement. I felt a commitment to test the ideas of equity, citizen participation and community action that so many of us had talked about. Maybe "I" and "we" could hold power in a more responsible, sensitive and humane manner than the people whom we had criticized for so long. Yet I was equally bound and felt committed to the requirements of the office I held.

For four years I moved back and forth between these allegiances. At times, I felt like a translator interpreting conflict-ing attitudes and at times I felt compelled to deflate people's expectations of myself and what they thought the 1960s were all about. A mythology has grown up about the '60s, the sort of instant history reached sometimes by *Newsweek* or *Time,* that makes the record of that period seem too neat and tidy.

Clearly something happened. A generation came of age at a time of immense prosperity. Demographically we broke the charts. Economically our feeding, housing and need to be educated made work for almost everybody in America. The cultural epicenter of our country moved from one generation to another. Most importantly, our education and idealism led us to question America's post-World War II vision that all Americans were white, middle-class or soon going to be, and owners of a half-acre lot in the suburbs.

That we had the opportunity to question was surely a gift from our parents. We had the luxury to be idealistic, a luxury no doubt that we got because our parents never had that luxury when they were growing up. Blacks and other poor people, out of necessity and their commitment to the American ideal, had to question and then shatter America's contented image of itself. Those of us coming out of college in the early '60s could afford to do it. We could afford to go to Mississippi for Freedom Summer. We could afford to take a semester off and become Appalachian

Volunteers. We knew that we could spend two years with the Peace Corps and indeed we were encouraged to do so. We were encouraged to be idealistic.

And so we were. One can look back a decade and say that we were truly a fortunate generation, maybe even spoiled. But one should also look back and say that we were patriotic and idealistic; young men and women of good intentions who wanted to make America better.

What really happened? Those of us who committed ourselves to a new and more democratic image of America soon found ourselves caught up in not one reform movement but many. Reform begat reform. Each movement spun off another. Everything was shared: tactics and strategy, office space and apartments, ideals and hopes. People coalesced around one cause only to go off to another. The movements innumerable became "The Movement." Capital M. America would move. America would be reformed.

No one can deny that Communists, Trotskyites and every other strand of leftist thinking had people participating in the Movement and in other reform efforts of the last decade, but so did large segments of the middle class and the business community. I remain convinced that the broad spectrum of people who supported the antiwar movement and other reform efforts, who wrote their congressmen, signed petitions and marched in support of causes wanted America to be the country we had been taught it already was.

I also cannot believe that we were duped or totally wrong in taking the positions we took during the war. More than once I have changed the opinions I held a decade ago. I find it impossible to be supportive of what Vietnam has done in Laos and what it did to the "boat people." I find it difficult to support Vietnam's domination of Cambodia, but find the alternative of supporting Pol Pot even worse. One cannot accuse America of being too militaristic without questioning what the Soviet Union has supported in Cambodia, what it did in Afghanistan and what it threatens to do in Poland.

But these changes reflect changes in attitude toward other nations, not toward America. Those of us who criticized America's involvement in Vietnam did so because we held America to a higher standard than that of the Soviet Union and Vietnam. That standard hasn't changed. Hans Morgenthau wrote in 1970 in *Truth and Power* that a country founded on Jeffersonian principles cannot long survive by using the methods of Bismarck to make its foreign policy succeed. The truth and power of that statement have not diminished in the last decade.

The legacy of Vietnam is easier to understand in terms of political reactions than it is in terms of the emotional upheaval the country endured and the sentiments that are held today by the American people about Vietnam. The loss of authority caused by the deception of the American people by two presidents is a source of distress for many, including myself. The possibility of a "lost generation" of voters seems very real and dangerous. No country can long survive if a significant portion of its citizens are unwilling to sanction the actions of its leaders.

How those in power come to terms with the issue of restoring that trust seems to me to be a critical issue of the 1980s. I see no indication that those now in power in Washington have any understanding of how to go about regaining that trust. Their desire to restore the old lines of authority without any sensitivity to the fundamental fracturing that took place seems to me to be at best a stopgap measure that is reassuring to an older generation but not to the country at large and to my generation in the specific.

The emotional wounds caused by conflict are more difficult to discern. One reads on occasion of the Vietnam veteran who suddenly goes berserk and one wonders whether it is a foreshadowing of something that the country at large has yet to go through. The Red Scare of the 1920s, the McCarthy purges of the 1950s and the Nixonian abuse of constitutional liberties, events that showed the worst side of the American character, were ugly political spasms that followed other conflicts that to some degree divided the country. At times I fear that an even larger spasm will be pushed upon the American public by conservatives determined to vindicate themselves. My nightmare is tempered by the knowledge that a majority of Americans have shown an extraordinary adaptability in coming to terms with the war. Reduced to cryptic statements about it being a "mistake" and a "waste," most Americans seem to have little desire to engage in witch-hunts.

I am also troubled by the sense of irresponsibility and cynicism which many people have about our obligations to freely serve others and to defend our common interests. As I traveled to college campuses in the fall of 1980, I frequently ran into people whose trip to the post office to register for the draft was their first act of citizenship and who were appalled when I told them that I favor not only registration but a military raised by equitable conscription and, moreover, that I believe in national service for both men and women.

My feelings toward members of my generation are different. We remain split from within and from the generations before and behind us. I feel a sense of separateness from those people of my age who simply responded to what they regarded as the nation's interest by going to war. I am pained by the personal stories of tragedy of Vietnam veterans. I do not think that they were foolish, stupid or criminals. Just used.

The split inherent in any generation between the classes, a split that our society has traditionally been able to keep indistinct, became pronounced and rigid, codified by the Selective Service classification system—I-A, 2-S, I-Y, 4-F. We all remember, don't we? Anyone who grew up during the war knows who went and who didn't. The poor, less-educated and lower-middle-class men went and those of us who were upper-middle-class and college-educated didn't. The fact that many of us didn't because we found it morally impossible does not negate the fact that one class of people was used while another remained privileged.

The knowledge that so many men of the upper middle class used the system to beat it only accentuates the divisions between men of my generation. I am saddened by the cynicism of the many people whose prime motivation for being involved in the antiwar movement was merely self-preservation. Once the heat of the draft had ended, they went on with the business of being stockbrokers or lawyers or whatever else they had hoped for in their lives.

For many of us who fought to end the war, it has taken over a decade to sort out what happened. The sifting and sorting has been intensely personal. For some men who opposed the war, the fact that they used the country's repugnance toward it to avoid the draft has left a residual guilt of not facing one's obligations. Only a few, like James Fallows, have had the integrity to speak openly about what has been on the minds of many.

For other men, not joining the Army left them with the distinct feeling that they had missed a critical "rite of passage" in coming to terms with their manhood. Understanding the long-term consequences of missing that ritual passage is beyond my capacity. But the fact that this feeling came at a time when the very idea of manhood was rightfully being challenged by the feminist movement has to be factored into any new conceptualization by our culture of what it means to be a man. This is a task that seems to me to be as profound as any we will face in the next ten years.

But for many more of us the "rite of passage" was met. Moral choices had to be made. Reduced to the abstractness of the Selective Service System's draft categories, the choices were nevertheless full of distinctions that were difficult to articulate but full of moral meaning to those who faced them squarely: to serve or not to serve; to avoid the draft by faking a medical or becoming a CO; to leave for Canada or to become a draft resister and face the possibility of jail; to demonstrate or not to demonstrate; to practice civil disobedience and face arrest or to avoid it. Finally, to face one's parents and peers once a decision had been made. That choices of a different nature but of equal seriousness were made by those who went to Vietnam I have no doubt.

The legacy of having to make such choices so early in one's life seems to me to be a capacity for tolerance and empathy by members of my generation for anyone, regardless of what side they chose, who made such decisions. I have found that people of my generation show such a tolerance for each other, an empathy that does not reach beyond generational lines when talking about the war. 'Nam is a generational talisman that only we can touch.

For those of us who actively dissented, the war has been the point around which we have pivoted our lives during the last decade. It shaped our attitudes and personal lives more than we ever imagined. Some of us had to overcome a deep suspicion and at times the justified paranoia that those in authority were systematically disrupting our lives. Parts of our lives were delayed because we felt compelled to commit ourselves to each new facet of the Movement. It is only now that we have begun picking up those pieces—buying houses, getting married, having children and settling on careers. A few of us "burnt out" and rejected everything about the political process. But many more of us, if we had an adverse reaction to the power of the federal government to do harm, turned that reaction into a positive commitment to make government more responsive to people where they live and work, at the local and state level.

Looking back on those years I see two aspects of the Vietnam era that are fundamentally positive for the future of this country: the capacity for self-criticism and the tolerance that people within my generation have developed. Our ability to rebuild a core vision of what we want our society to be in the future rests largely on our ability to use these capacities in a positive way.

I see little indication that those who hold power now will do so. It may be that developing a new vision of what our society should be, one that encapsulates a richer understanding of patriotism, our obligations to each other and to the world, will have to wait until we are in our political majority a decade hence.

People have a tendency to look upon our generation as one that is already politically spent, to see us as part of history. I don't believe that to be the case. They forget that we were all in our early twenties when we did what we had to do in the '60s. Our real influence as a generation has yet to be felt.

CHAPTER TWELVE

Women and the War

Susan Jacoby

"TALKING ABOUT THE VIETNAM WAR AND WOMEN IS like talking about the effect of jogging on cripples," a 36-year-old political scientist said when I told him I was writing about the ways in which the Vietnam era had changed the lives of American women and relations between the sexes.

This extraordinary pronouncement was uttered by a man who—like millions of white, draft-age men during the Vietnam years—sat out the war in college and graduate school with a student deferment. "We had to make a moral choice about the war," he argued, "and women didn't." All wars produce their quota of mythic nonsense and Vietnam—appropriately enough for a war fought not by a majority but by a minority—has produced the saga of the conscience-stricken young man who made the agonizing choice to stay home in the classroom while his brothers fought in the jungles of Southeast Asia.

This myth may have been a reality for the few who were seriously involved in resistance to the draft, draft counseling and antiwar organization, but it was not true for the many. I am a 35-year-old white woman and a journalist, which means that—had I been a man subject to the draft—I probably would have stayed in school longer instead of going to work as a reporter for *The Washington Post* in 1965. Like me, most of the young men and women I knew during the Vietnam era were somewhat opposed to the war in its early years and became more opposed as the casualties mounted with no end in sight in the late 1960s. I don't recall a single discussion with a man about whether it was "right" or "wrong" to wangle a deferment; the only question for most men was whether or not it was possible to legally avoid the draft.

I understand why some men of my generation prefer to remember things the way they weren't. I, too, feel a searing shame whenever I see pictures of crippled Vietnam veterans But shame and guilt are notorious impediments to accurate historical memory. Most of us at home, regardless of our sex, didn't spend a great deal of time thinking about or doing anything to bring an end to the war. We were against the war, but we didn't put much of ourselves on the line in the cause. *That* is something to be ashamed of, but the real issue is only obscured by pious mouthings from men about the "painful" moral choice of getting a student deferment.

It has been said before, but it is worth saying again: Vietnam was a war fought by a small proportion of the population, especially in comparison with the gigantic, near-universal manpower effort that supported the Second World War. The combat effort in Vietnam was based not only on a numerical minority but on economic and racial minorities—the poor, those without high school diplomas, blacks, Hispanics, rural whites. During the Vietnam period, approximately 25 million men came of draft age. An estimated 9.3 million served in some branch of the military, and 3.1 million were actually in Southeast Asia. To put it another way, only one out of every eight draft-age men saw action in Vietnam—and the proportion of black and Hispanic soldiers in combat was much higher than in the Army as a whole. When people of my generation talk to our parents—the World War II generation now in its fifties and sixties—we invariably find that our fathers were on active duty and our mothers were keeping the economy going at home. When we talk to our own grandchildren 20 or 30 years from now, they are apt to find that both Grandma and Grandpa were safe at home during the Vietnam years.

During the Vietnam era, there was a commonality of experience between the sexes—at least in middle-class America—that did not exist in any previous war. It is ironic that this common experience has helped produce more lasting changes in economic, political and social relationships between women and men than the radically different experiences of the sexes during other wars. There is no single explanation for these changes; they emerged from structural employment shifts that were accelerated by the wartime economy and from the social upheaval generated first by the antiwar movement and then by the feminist movement.

In wars involving most of the able-bodied male population, the classic economic pattern is for women to take over civilian jobs until the men return home. That is what happened after World War II, when a generation of Rosie-the-Riveters left the job market to produce the epic postwar baby boom. The role of women in the Vietnam period was entirely different. There was a tremendous expansion of employment opportunities for everyone, fueled not only by military spending but by a consumer boom unprecedented in wartime economies. Wars generally place the consumer sector of an economy on an austerity basis. During World War II, Americans (who looked like and were millionaires in comparison with the inhabitants of ruined Europe) still went without butter and rubber and nylon. During the Vietnam era, Americans enjoyed a prosperity that is unique in the history of modern war. One structural change of particular importance for women was the rapid growth in the service and retailing sectors of the economy.

The women who joined the labor force during the Vietnam years did not see themselves primarily as (and in fact were not) substitutes for men who were in the military. They were working because the economy was booming, because the most significant expansion of jobs had occurred in service and retailing fields most hospitable to women, and—last but not least—because the emerging feminist movement was beginning to provide cultural support for women who wanted to work outside their homes. Statistics tell the story: In 1960, only one out of five married women had a job. By 1970, the proportion had risen to one in three. Now more than half of married women—and a much larger proportion of all women between college graduation and retirement age—are at work. There was no drop in female employment when the Vietnam War ended. The inflation of the late 1970s was, of course, a vital factor keeping women in the labor force, but the trend was established long before the two-income household became an economic necessity for many families.

The emergence of the feminist movement during the latter half of the war was, I believe, a crucial factor in stemming any "back-to-the-home" impulses on the part of women (and their men). Returning veterans whose wives had originally gone to work with the classic intention of "filling in" for their absent husbands found that the attitudes of their women had altered radically. I know one ambitious woman who went to work in 1968 as a legal secretary to save money for her husband's college tuition. By the time he completed his three-year tour of duty in the Army, she had decided she wanted to go to law school. They are still paying off the loans they took out to finance both of their educations.

This story offers an almost too-neat example of the changes in the status of women that took place in the later years of the Vietnam War and the early years of the feminist movement, but it does illustrate a general pattern. Between 1965 and 1970, the growth of female employment was the product of a burgeoning economy and was confined primarily to female-dominated occupations. After 1970, the feminist movement spurred the entry of more women into traditionally male-dominated professions and some blue-collar unions.

Wartime male displacement from the civilian economy was only one factor—and not the most important one—in this process. In the first place, most of the men who served in the military during the Vietnam era were only in uniform for two years—a sharp contrast with World War II, when every man was in the service for the duration. Secondly, a disproportionate segment of the Vietnam army was poor and undereducated. There were no jobs for many of these men before they entered the military and—to their sadness and bitterness—there were no jobs for them when they got out.

Many men with student deferments did stay in school longer

than they would have if there had been no war, but there is little evidence that this phenomenon had any real impact on the entry of women into professions. The proportion of women in professional schools and professional jobs increased most dramatically not during but after the war. The feminist movement—not the war—was responsible for the admission of more women to law and medical schools in the 1970s. Before 1970, most professional schools had quotas restricting the admission of women, just as they had quotas limiting the enrollment of Jews until the 1950s.

The political impact of the Vietnam era on women, like the economic impact, can only be understood in terms of a continuum that includes the civil rights movement of the early 1960s, the antiwar movement of the late '60s and the feminist movement of the '70s. Many men, including some perceptive historians and political analysts, still do not realize that politically conscious feminism emerged from both the civil rights and antiwar efforts. Colorado's Rep. Patricia Schroeder described the connection this way: "One of the reasons I got mad enough to run was that I had a congressman who didn't have time to talk to me about the Vietnam War but who had time to send me complimentary cookbooks and baby books."

For a core of politically active women, feminism emerged from the contradiction between professed ideals of social justice and the misogyny of many men (black and white) in the civil rights and antiwar movements. The men in the civil rights movement administered the first shock to many women who had volunteered for dangerous duty in the Deep South because they believed in equal rights for everyone. One woman who ran a freedom school in Mississippi in the early 1960s remembers her chagrin at the failure of her superiors to replace a local director whose drinking habits were literally endangering the lives of volunteer workers. She was the only replacement available at the time, and the state supervisor told her bluntly that "any man—black or white, drunk or sober—can run things better than any woman." Stokely Carmichael's famous statement that "the only position for women in our movement is prone" is not an apocryphal story.

During the civil rights years, women kept quiet. It seemed trivial to complain about sex discrimination when people were risking their lives in the cause of justice. The antiwar movement, however, sharpened women's perceptions of inequity between the sexes. The movement was definitely not an equal opportunity employer. The leadership—candidates, speakers at rallies, most of the defendants in celebrated cases—was male. (Jane Fonda doesn't count; as an entertainer with a famous name, she was exempt from the usual rules of the game.)

Women were the support system of the peace movement—the volunteers who made telephone calls, mailed out fliers and ordered doughnuts, coffee and stronger libations. (I remember covering an antiwar protest where one of the organizers' girl friends was sent out to buy marijuana.)

The position of women in the antiwar movement of the late '60s was no different from that of women in corporations, financial institutions and universities. But that was just the point: Women who had become involved in social protest because they believed in justice were sensitive to the contradiction between egalitarian ideals and the reality of male dominance and priv- ilege—whether it was clothed in a denim jacket or a three-piece gabardine suit.

In the late 1960s, a group of West Coast antiwar activists posed for a famous picture in which the men, brandishing grenades and bricks and lead pipes, glowered at several cowering women. One of the men had his foot planted atop the hugely swollen belly of the mother-to-be who was lying on the floor. All in good fun. The photograph was made into a poster, presumably intended to convey the message that war was bad for women, children and all living things.

The only message that picture conveyed to me, when it crossed my desk as a press release in the *Post* newsroom, was the degradation of a pregnant woman. This was long before feminism had surfaced as a distinct social force, but I remember thinking that something was radically wrong with a bunch of people who would use the image of a supine woman's body in such a way. Several years later, when some of the "girls" who had been cooks and typists and envelope stuffers of the antiwar movement had emerged as adult leaders of the feminist movement, I realized how deeply my generation of women had been affected by the macho attitudes they found in the ostensibly egalitarian world of antiwar protest. (As a reporter and in my personal life, I have found this sort of macho to be much more common among men who spent the war at home than among those who actually fought in Vietnam. I have often wondered whether the millions of men my age who avoided the draft may feel "unmanned" in a way that no woman can truly understand.)

There was also a positive side to the experience of women in antiwar politics—experience that was first put to use by feminists and then by the new generation of women seeking political office. The women's movement, like the peace movement, derived a large measure of its success from the ability to reach—and move—people who had not been galvanized by other political and social issues.

Eugene J. McCarthy's 1968 presidential primary campaign in New Hampshire, which persuaded President Johnson not to seek reelection, owed its success to the door-to-door efforts of volunteers and to a large number of small financial contributions. This effort has been imitated repeatedly, with modifications and improvements, by candidates who lack a traditional power base. Nearly all of the young women who were first elected to office in the '70s—at the local, state or national level—fit that description perfectly.

Politically active women were, of course, more directly affected by the experience of the antiwar movement and feminism than the female population as a whole, but there is considerable evidence of an intricate and long-lasting effect on women as voters. Marjorie Lansing, a professor of political science at Eastern Michigan University, has compiled a study of long-term voting patterns showing that women have consistently been more opposed than men to increased defense spending, the draft, and the use of military force. Among no group of women is this phenomenon more evident than those under 40—the generation that matured during the Vietnam era.

In examining the data, it is startling to see that women in their thirties are more opposed than men of the same age to draft registration and to any eventual reinstatement of the draft. Men now in their thirties and forties were, after all, the ones who bore the burden of fighting an unpopular war or—for the majority—the knowledge that they had avoided the burden. Nevertheless, in 1969 more than 64 percent of women but only 48 percent of men in a Gallup Poll ranked themselves as "doves."

In 1980 the difference in the percentage of men and women who voted for Ronald Reagan was substantial. More than 54 percent of men, and only 47 percent of women, voted for Reagan. The men in the Vietnam generation voted for Reagan in the same proportion as men of other ages. In the months following the election, a number of pollsters found that women's fears of a more "hawkish" policy were a more important factor in their distrust of Reagan than his opposition to the Equal Rights Amendment. The statistics are clear on one point: If the American electorate had been made up entirely of women, Ronald Reagan would not have been elected president.

A possible restoration of the draft in the 1980s would pose a substantial political and intellectual dilemma for many women who were shaped by both the antiwar and feminist movements.

It is obviously inconsistent to support equal rights for women and a military draft limited to men. Women's groups, as well as women officeholders strongly identified with feminism, did not have to face the issue squarely when President Carter asked for a resumption of draft registration. Most feminists were against draft registration for *anyone*, regarding it as a sneaky first step toward a real draft.

Women will not find the issue as easy to resolve if there is a real move toward resumption of compulsory peacetime military service. Feminists who emerged from the antiwar movement (and, if the Lansing study is accurate, a majority of all women) tend to oppose any military conscription in peacetime. But what if a president asks for a resumption of the draft and Congress accedes to the request?

The issue is further complicated by the ultimate fate of the Equal Rights Amendment. If the ERA has not been ratified, it is difficult to imagine that any major women's organization would support the inclusion of women in a draft. If the ERA were ratified, however, it would be difficult to defend the exclusion of women from the draft. It might also be unconstitutional. Over the years, supporters of the ERA have done their cause a disservice by evading the issue and saying that Congress already has the power to draft women. Of course Congress has the power, but the ERA would probably make it impossible for Congress to enact a draft for one sex.

Women in Congress—including those who regard requests for increased military expenditures with great skepticism—have paid considerable attention to improving opportunities for women and ending sex discrimination in the volunteer army. The expanded opportunities for women in the volunteer army have proved a boon to girls from poor families, who have used the armed services—as poor young men did a generation or two ago—to gain education and job training they would not otherwise have received.

Support for equal opportunity in a volunteer army is a logical position for a woman who is unalterably opposed to any peacetime draft. But I have serious reservations about this position (an attitude I share with a number of generals, though my reasons are different). My belief that the Vietnam War was a mistake is, in ironic fashion, responsible for my doubts about the role of a volunteer army in a democratic society. I believe the single most important element prolonging the war was the fact that it was fought by a minority, while the majority was able to avoid the draft. There is no question in my mind that a universal draft would have led to a much earlier examination of our role in Vietnam. Today, the volunteer army is even more of a minority military force than the Vietnam army was. Blacks, Hispanics and the poor are disproportionately represented. Young men (and women) from comfortable backgrounds are not eager to serve Uncle Sam.

I believe the United States does need a peacetime army and that ill-advised military adventures are much more likely if the burden is not shared equally by all classes in society. The burden can never be fairly distributed in a society with a volunteer army or an inequitable draft like the one that existed during the Vietnam years. If I were pressed to the wall—as politicians might be in the 1980s—I would have to say that the country should have a universal service lottery including both men and women.

The possibility of women in combat is a more complicated issue. During the Vietnam War, most men in the military were *not* in combat. It seems clear that a wide variety of noncombat duties can be performed equally well by both sexes, but combat is another matter. I would expect the proportion of women who could physically qualify for combat to be much smaller than the proportion of men. Unfair, true, but not as unfair as exempting women from service altogether. And who can deny that there is a kind of biological insanity in sending women into combat?

The whole issue makes women uncomfortable, but there is no way around it unless you believe there is no need for an army. It makes men uncomfortable too. Some men who complain loudly about the exemption of women from the draft are equally horrified at the suggestion that *some* women might make good combat soldiers. This reaction may be part male chauvinism, but it is also rooted in a profoundly protective biological instinct. If we lose all awareness of the role of women as potential child-bearers, what sort of a society will be left to defend?

One issue that has lingered after the Vietnam War is less complicated. It is the matter of veterans' preference, a system adopted at the end of World War II in which men who have served in the military receive priority for a wide variety of jobs in the federal government. Similar systems exist in most state and local governments. Feminist organizations, notably the National Organization for Women, are totally opposed to any form of veterans' preference. I agree with their general position—with the exception of veterans who were disabled in combat.

The veterans' preference system, which benefits all men who have served in the military—in peace or war, combat or noncombat positions—has been a long-term source of discrimination against women in public employment. President Carter tried to abolish it in the late 1970s and got nowhere in Congress.

The rationale for veterans' preference is that the country owes something to men who risked their lives in the service. The result has been that millions of able-bodied men—many of them veterans of the peacetime army between the end of Korea and the beginning of Vietnam—have been able to obtain priority for Civil Service jobs 5, 10, 15, 20 years after leaving the service. Vietnam veterans, with their disproportionate representation from the ranks of poor minorities, have benefited the least from veterans' preference. The continuation of such preference will not help them in the job market. The real scandal of America's treatment of returning Vietnam veterans has been the government's failure to provide educational benefits comparable to those offered veterans of previous wars.

My own views on the military, particularly on the matter of a peacetime draft, are not typical of women as a group (if there is a typical group of women). For many women who came to maturity during the Vietnam era, anything connected with the military can be a bitter pill to swallow. This is true not only of middle-class women who were heavily represented in the ranks of antiwar protesters, but of poorer women whose men were drafted and sent to Vietnam. I recently interviewed a black woman whose husband was killed in Vietnam in 1967, and her views reflect those of many women of differing backgrounds. She was disturbed because her 17-year-old daughter wanted to enlist in the Army upon graduation from high school.

"I told my girl I can't run her life," she said. "The Army can pay for schooling I can't afford. And her daddy, he'd probably be the first one to say go ahead. He enlisted himself and I told him then he was crazy. Maybe you think I'm talking like this just because her daddy died in the Army. I don't really think my girl is going to be sent into action and killed, but somehow I just don't want her to have anything to do with it. The right to shoot somebody is an equal right I can do without. Like that song the kids used to sing—'Ain't gonna study war no more.' Makes sense to me still."

CHAPTER THIRTEEN

We've Adjusted Too Well

Tim O'Brien

CONTRARY TO POPULAR STEREOTYPES, MOST VIET-
nam veterans have made the adjustment to peace. Granted, many
of us continue to suffer, but the vast majority are *not* hooked on
drugs, *not* unemployed, are *not* suicidal, are *not* beating up wives
and children, are *not* robbing banks, are *not* knee-deep in grief or
self-pity or despair.

Like our fathers, we came home from war to pursue careers
and loves and cars and houses and dollars and vacations and all
the pleasures of peace. Who can blame us? Wasn't peace the
purpose? Peace with honor and dignity. Hadn't we sacrificed
years of our lives? On the battlefield, weren't our daydreams lush
with images of peace? And here at home, weren't the shrinks and
scriptwriters and politicians telling us, at least by implication,
that we *ought* to be seeking social and psychological readjustment? Heal the wounds, pick up the pieces.

Well, we've done it. By and large we've succeeded. And
that's the problem. We've adjusted too well.

In our pursuit of peaceful, ordinary lives, too many of us
have lost touch with the horror of war. Too many have forgotten—
misplaced, repressed, chosen to ignore—the anguish that once
dominated our lives. The guilt, the fear, the painful urgencies
have faded.

That's sad. We should remember. Not in a crippling, de-
bilitating way, but rather a form of affirmation: Yes, war is hell.
The cliché is true. Oh, we all *know* it's true, we know it in an
abstract way, the way we know that the moon is a lonely place.
But soldiers, having been there, have witnessed the particulars
which give validity and meaning to the abstract. That's an
important kind of knowledge, for it reminds us of the stakes:

human lives, human limbs. Real lives, real limbs. Nothing abstract.

It would seem that the memories of soldiers should serve, at least in a modest way, as a restraint on national bellicosity. But time and distance erode memory. We adjust, we lose the intensity. We look back on our own histories with a kind of numb disbelief, as though none of it really happened, as if paging through a scrapbook of photographs without being able to recollect the circumstances and colors and emotions at the moment the shutter clicked. Filters are placed over memory. For many of us, years later, Vietnam is seen with a certain tempered nostalgia. A half-remembered adventure. We feel, many of us, vaguely proud at having "been there," forgetting the terror, straining out the bad stuff, focusing on the afterimage.

The same principle, I think, applies for the population as a whole, veterans and nonveterans. We have forgotten, or lost the energy to recall, the terribly complex and ambiguous issues of the Vietnam War. Often with nostalgia, we look back on the turbulent years of the last decade, but we've ceased to think and talk seriously about those matters for which we once felt such passion. What to fight for? When, if ever, to use armed force as instruments of foreign policy? Which regimes to support, and how, and under what conditions? To what extent and by what means do we, as a nation, try to make good on our beliefs and principles—opposing tyranny, preserving freedoms, resisting aggression?

We used to *care* about these things. We paid attention, we debated, passion was high. These and other questions, philosophical and empirical, were at once more difficult and more urgent than they seem now. Fuzzily, we recall the outlines and the bare silhouettes of the issues, but we do not, I fear, recall much of the detail. We are left with impressions. Black and white, hawk and dove—the old categories. The national memory, like the memory of soldiers, is fickle and too damn short. Look around. Too many of us call for blood in every foreign crisis, but without any systematic examination of the implications of such action, without much inquiry into the history of American involvement in that part of the world, dumbly, blindly, impatiently.

We've all adjusted. The whole country. And I fear that we are back where we started.

I wish we were more troubled.

CHAPTER FOURTEEN

The Post-Vietnam Generation

Nicholas Lemann

I WAS BORN IN 1954, WHICH MAKES ME ABOUT 10 years younger than the other contributors to this book and, I suppose, a member of the post-Vietnam generation. Here is how the war directly touched my life: I registered for the draft when I turned 18, and the following year I was given the lottery number of six. I remember summoning forth in myself at the time some mixture of panic and self-pity, but given the capacities of a 19-year-old in that department it was pretty halfhearted. It was 1973, and I knew in my heart that I wasn't going to be called. I filed a perfunctory request with my draft board for conscientious objector status because that was what one did, and was turned down. As I recall it, the draft board said that my application seemed to be born out of convenience. That was perfectly true; I didn't object; and a few weeks later the draft was ended. That's my experience with the Vietnam War.

But of course there is more to it than that. Mostly because of Vietnam and the attitudes it produced toward military service, of all my friends and acquaintances of my own age, only one has been in the armed forces. He left college to join the Marines and everybody said it was just because he was having an identity crisis. I grew up with a complete ignorance of and hostility toward the American military. When I was a teenager I assumed without even thinking about it that there was something wrong, even pathological, with anyone who was in the service. Soon after I started working as a reporter I was assigned a story about the Army, and I remember the first officer I interviewed looking at me in amazement when I asked him which was the higher rank, captain or major.

And there is more to it than that. Mostly because of Vietnam,

I grew up regarding every American president in my lifetime as a pathological war criminal. Eisenhower was a general—what further proof was needed? Kennedy got us into Vietnam. Johnson started the escalation and the bombing. Nixon said he had a secret plan to end the war and then kept it going for five years after his election. Naturally this attitude on my part logically extended itself, so that I also believed, as did my friends, that America could do nothing right; that it was a force of evil in the world; that, therefore, the country's leadership was also stupid and venal (hadn't it produced all those evil presidents?); and that the whole idea of order and authority was probably wrong too. I can remember two political events in college that caused people to go out in the streets on warm nights, whooping and yelling with joy: the resignation of President Nixon and the fall of the government of South Vietnam to the Communists.

Unlike the other contributors to this book, I am not someone to whom the idea that our country and its dominant institutions were deeply and fundamentally flawed was a dramatic revelation. It was what I grew up on. My first political memory is of the principal of my school calling an assembly to tell us that the Cubans might send missiles our way. My second political memory is of the principal calling us together again a year later to tell us that President Kennedy had been killed. I cannot remember having any perception of the Vietnam War other than it was a bad war that we were losing. I cannot remember ever not thinking of the incumbent president as a failure. And I should stress that I grew up in a conservative southern city, rather than some hotbed of chic anti-Americanism. Most of my childhood friends are now businessmen and housewives, radical by no stretch of the imagination. What makes us all enormously different from our parents is not the way we live our lives, but the assumptions that lie behind the way we live: not patriotism but cynicism. Everything is pretty much the same on the surface. Underneath, everything is different. We have no center. Our parents did.

This is not completely the fault of Vietnam. For a variety of reasons, a setting was created in the years following World War II through which Vietnam's ripples were able to move with particular force, more so than would have been possible a generation earlier. The affluence of the postwar years brought with it an optimism in which a major disappointment was likely to be especially keenly felt. The affluence—and, along with it, the absolute preeminence of large institutions in American life— made the population more mobile and much more suburban. As a result, the things that traditionally gave American life its center— religion, community, the extended family and, as the years wore on, even marriage—all began to erode. Instead, the center became an idea about America. When events began to contradict the idea, there was suddenly nothing to fall back on.

So people like me assumed that the enterprise was not noble, rebelled against it for a time, and then joined it, not out of the sincere belief of our parents, but because there was no other choice. That's why today, although we're better educated than they were, we vote less. It's why survey after survey shows us to feel no loyalty to our employers. It's why marriage and children scare us. There is no large example from our lives that shows us connections like these producing anything but pain. So we stay loose and free and that way at least stave off being disappointed. How could anyone have actually believed in Vietnam? In a president? In the idea that the nation occupied some moral higher ground? Those who did certainly looked silly to us.

On the morning after the unsuccessful American raid on Iran in the spring of 1980, my editor asked me to write a story about, as he put it, "how it feels." He didn't mean how it felt to me. He said it was a sad day for the flag and that I should try to find a way to convey some of that. So I went out and interviewed people standing in line for the White House tour, and made some phone calls, and did all the other things I was supposed to do, and when I sat down to write it, I couldn't. That had never happened to me before, and it felt terrible, but the fact was that I didn't know "how it feels" in anything close to the way I knew my editor meant it. The idea of an American defeat just didn't have any special resonance for me. The America I grew up with was always a loser.

When that is the way you are, how do you conduct your life? What happens next? I can answer that best by an analogy. Let's say you didn't believe in love. You knew that other people did, but you simply didn't. You could then go about your business accordingly, staying on the surface of things, avoiding deep involvements. This, in my analogy, would correspond to moving to New Hampshire or some similar locale that held the promise of escape from the passions of society; many of my contemporaries have done that. Or you could, to continue the analogy, decide to behave as if there were such a thing as love even though you didn't believe it, just because that is how the world is organized and therefore doing so makes it easier to get along. By that I mean, in the larger sense, that you could get a respectable job, remain perfectly normal to outward appearances, and in that way keep your lack of belief a little secret all your own.

Or, finally, you could, rather than assuming that love really existed, merely leave yourself open to it as a possibility and let it come along, if it did exist. For most people, after all, it does sooner or later. In that way, if love—or, to draw out the analogy again, patriotism or commitment or belief—came, it would hit you with the drama of a brand-new discovery, the way the discovery that fire is hot must hit a baby. The baby is too young to know intellectually or instinctively that fire is hot, so to him it is a wild revelation, and one that does him a lot of good. People like me are no longer babies, but verities that might seem equally elementary strike us with that same force. Is it possible actually to care who is elected president? What the fate of our community will be? About our work? About love? About American hostages in Iran? To our great surprise, it is; and to our further surprise, caring deeply about those things lends to life a gravity and meaning that enriches it beyond measure. They must sound silly to older people, these little revelations of ours. They must make you think we're spoiled brats, as I know many of you think many of us are. But to us, they provide the only moral course by which to live, and laughing at them is like laughing at the joy an accident victim feels after his first halting steps.

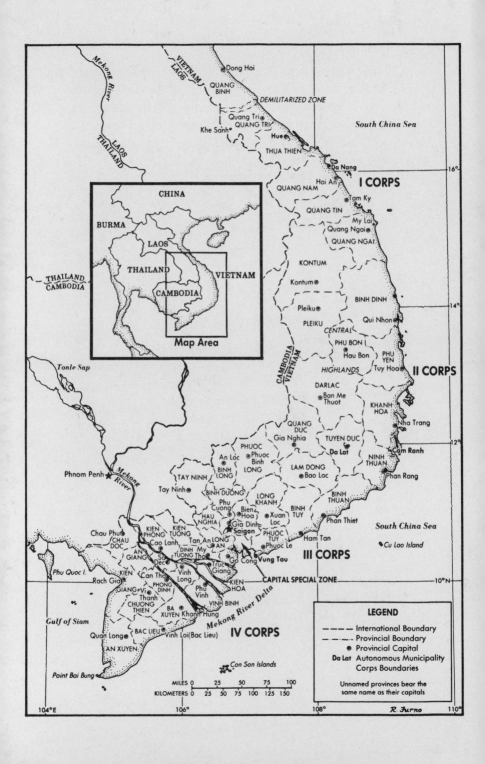

CHRONOLOGY

This is a chronology of the American involvement in Vietnam, adapted from a study prepared by the Congressional Research Service of the Library of Congress and the staff of the Senate Foreign Relations Committee:

1955

January 1: United States begins direct aid to government of South Vietnam.

February 12: U.S. Military Assistance Advisory Group (MAAG) takes over training of South Vietnamese Army from the French.

February 19: Southeast Asia Collective Defense Treaty (SEATO) comes into force.

October 26: Republic of Vietnam is proclaimed, with Ngo Dinh Diem as first president.

1956

July 6: Vice President Richard M. Nixon visits Saigon, carrying letter from President Eisenhower to President Diem.

1957

May 11: President Diem visits Washington, issues joint communiqué with President Eisenhower declaring that both countries will work toward "peaceful unification" of North and South Vietnam.

October 22: U.S. MAAG and U.S. Information Service installations in Saigon are bombed; U.S. personnel injured.

1959

May: U.S. Pacific Command directs U.S. advisers be provided to South Vietnamese infantry regiments and artillery, armored and Marine battalions.

July 8: Communist guerrillas attack Vietnamese base at Bien Hoa, killing two U.S. military advisers.

1960

February 5: South Vietnam asks United States to double MAAG strength to 685.

May 5: United States announces MAAG will be doubled by year's end.

May 30: U.S. Special Forces team arrives in Vietnam to conduct training.

June–October: Communist guerrilla activities in South Vietnam increase.

November 11–12: Military coup attempt fails to overthrow President Diem.

1961

January 29: Radio Hanoi announces establishment in December 1960 of National Front for Liberation of South Vietnam.

March 10: National Front announces guerrilla offensive to prevent presidential elections scheduled for April.

April 3: U.S.–South Vietnamese Treaty of Amity and Economic Relations signed in Saigon.

May 5: President Kennedy warns that U.S. combat forces may have to be used to save South Vietnam from communism.

May 13: Joint U.S.–South Vietnamese communiqué issued during visit to Saigon by Vice President Lyndon B. Johnson pledges additional U.S. military and economic aid.

October 11: President Kennedy sends his military adviser, Gen. Maxwell Taylor, to investigate military situation in South Vietnam.

October 18: President Diem declares state of emergency in South Vietnam.

December 8: State Department "white paper" warns South Vietnam is threatened by "clear and present danger" of communist conquest.

December 14: President Kennedy pledges increased aid to South Vietnam

1962

February 7: Two U.S. Army air support companies arrive in Saigon, increasing total of U.S. military personnel in South Vietnam to 4,000.

February 8: U.S. Military Assistance Command, Vietnam (MACV) established in Saigon, under Gen. Paul D. Harkins.

September 12: Gen. Maxwell Taylor visits Central Highlands where U.S. Special Forces are training *montagnards* for war against Viet Cong guerrillas.

December 29: Saigon announces that 39 percent of South Vietnam's population is now living in fortified "strategic hamlets."

1963

January 2–3: Three Americans killed as Viet Cong guerrillas defeat Vietnamese Army units at Ap Bac in Mekong Delta.

May 8: Twelve persons killed in riot in Hue during celebration of Buddha's birthday, touching off months of rioting and antigovernment demonstrations throughout South Vietnam.

August 26: Henry Cabot Lodge arrives in Saigon as U.S. ambassador, replacing Frederick Nolting.

September 2: President Kennedy declares in CBS television interview that the war cannot be won without support of South Vietnamese people "and, in my opinion in the last two months, the government has gotten out of touch with the people."

September 24–October 1: Secretary of Defense Robert S. McNamara and Gen. Maxwell Taylor visit South Vietnam to review war effort, report U.S. will continue support.

November 1: Military coup overthrows Diem government. Diem and his brother, Ngo Dinh Nhu, assassinated.

November 4: United States recognizes new government in Saigon.

November 22: President Kennedy assassinated.

November 24: President Lyndon Johnson announces U.S. will continue support of South Vietnam.

1964

January 30: Saigon government overthrown in military coup.

February 4–6: Viet Cong launch offensive in Tay Ninh province and Mekong Delta.

June 20: Gen. William C. Westmoreland takes command of MACV.

June 23: Gen. Maxwell Taylor is named ambassador to Saigon.

August 2: U.S. destroyer *Maddox* attacked in Gulf of Tonkin by North Vietnamese torpedo boats.

August 4: The *Maddox* and a second destroyer, USS *C. Turner Joy*, report another PT boat attack. President Johnson orders retaliatory air raids against North Vietnamese bases.

August 7: Congress passes Gulf of Tonkin Resolution supporting presidential authority to repel attacks against U.S. forces and declaring that U.S. will provide assistance in national defense to any SEATO member state that requests aid. Vote is 88 to 2 in Senate, 416 to 0 in House.

December 31: First North Vietnamese Army regulars enter South Vietnam. U.S. military strength reaches 23,000.

1965

February 7: Eight Americans killed, 109 wounded in Viet Cong mortar attack on base at Pleiku. President Johnson orders bombing of North Vietnam.

February 10: Viet Cong blow up U.S. barracks at Qui Nhon; 23 Americans killed.

February 28: U.S. and South Vietnam announce bombing of North Vietnam will continue in order to bring a negotiated settlement.

March 8: First American combat units (3,500 Marines) land at Da Nang.

March 19: First U.S. Army battalion arrives.

March 24: First college teach-in on the war held at University of Michigan.

April 7: President Johnson, in speech at Johns Hopkins University, proposes negotiations to end war, offers $1 billion in aid for Southeast Asia.

April 8: North Vietnam denounces Johnson speech, offers own four-point plan to end war.

May 4: President Johnson asks $700 million in additional defense funds for Vietnam. Bill is passed by House, 408 to 7, and by Senate, 88 to 3.

May 15: National teach-in against the war held in Washington and on college campuses.

June 7: U.S. troop level passes 50,000.

June 8: State Department spokesman says U.S. command has authority to send American troops into combat.

June 27: 173rd Airborne Brigade opens first major U.S. combat offensive.

July 8: White House announces resignation of Gen. Maxwell Taylor as ambassador to Saigon, to be replaced by Henry Cabot Lodge.

October 14: Defense Department announces December draft call of 45,224 men, largest since Korean War.

October 15–16: Antiwar demonstrations held in U.S. cities.

October 23: U.S. troop strength reaches 148,300.

December 15: Air Force planes destroy North Vietnamese power plant in first bomb raid on major industrial target.

1966

March 2: U.S. troop strength reaches 215,000.

April 12: B52s from Guam bomb North Vietnam for first time.

June 29: Hanoi and Haiphong oil installations bombed for first time.

December 31: U.S. troop strength reaches 389,000.

1967

January 25: Defense Department estimates Vietnam spending for fiscal year ending June 30 at $19.4 billion.

March 15: Nomination of Ellsworth Bunker to replace Henry Cabot Lodge as ambassador to Saigon announced by President Johnson.

April 15: Antiwar demonstrations held in New York and San Francisco.

July 15: Viet Cong mortar attack on U.S. air base at Da Nang kills 13 Americans, wounds 150.

August 3: President Johnson announces maximum limit on U.S. troops in Vietnam has been raised to 525,000.

August 17: Under Secretary of State Nicholas Katzenbach tells Senate that 1964 Gulf of Tonkin resolution gave president authority to commit troops without formal declaration of war.

September 3: South Vietnam holds presidential elections. Gen. Nguyen Van Thieu wins presidency with about 35 percent of the vote.

September 7: Defense Secretary McNamara announces U.S. will build anti-infiltration barrier along demilitarized zone between North and South Vietnam.

September 29: President Johnson, in San Antonio speech, announces U.S. will stop bombing North Vietnam "when this will lead promptly to productive discussions."

October 16: Public burning of 50 draft cards in Boston.

October 21: Antiwar demonstrators march on the Pentagon.

December 31: U.S. troops killed in combat during year total 9,378.

1968

January: North Vietnamese troops surround Marine base at Khe Sanh.

January 30–31: Communists launch Tet Offensive with attacks on major cities and province capitals. Viet Cong invade U.S. Embassy grounds in Saigon.

February 24: South Vietnamese recapture royal palace at Hue after 25 days of fighting.

March 16: U.S. troops report killing 128 enemy in hamlet called My Lai 4.

March 31: President Johnson orders partial halt of bombing of North Vietnam above 20th parallel and announces he will not run for reelection.

April 3: North Vietnam offers to discuss starting peace talks.

April 6: Relief forces reach Khe Sanh, ending 77-day siege.

April 10: Gen. Creighton Abrams named to replace Gen. Westmoreland as U.S. commander in Vietnam.

May 13: First negotiating session between U.S. and North Vietnam held in Paris.

June 27: U.S. forces withdraw from Khe Sanh.

August 8: Republican Party nominates Richard Nixon for president. Platform calls for "progressive de-Americanization" of the war and "a fair and equitable settlement."

August 28: Democrats nominate Vice President Hubert Humphrey for president, after Chicago convention marked by demonstrations and rioting in streets.

October 31: President Johnson announces total halt of bombing of North Vietnam.

November 1: North Vietnam announces Paris peace talks will be expanded to include South Vietnam and National Liberation Front on Nov. 6.

November 2: President Thieu says South Vietnam will not attend Paris peace talks.

November 6: Richard Nixon elected president.

December 31: U.S. troops killed in combat during year total 14,592.

1969

January 5: Henry Cabot Lodge named chief negotiator to Paris talks, replacing Averell Harriman.

February 23–24: Communist forces launch mortar and rocket attacks on 115 targets in South Vietnam.

May 12–13: Communists launch more than 200 attacks against military and civilian targets.

May 14: President Nixon offers eight-point formula for peace.

June 8: Presidents Nixon and Thieu meet on Midway Island. Nixon announces first U.S. troop withdrawal of 25,000 men.

September 16: President Nixon announces second U.S. troop withdrawal of 35,000 men by December 15.

October 4: Gallup Poll reports 58 percent of Americans polled feel U.S. involvement in war is a mistake.

October 15: Vietnam Moratorium demonstrations held across United States.

November 11: Veterans Day rallies held to support government policy on war.

November 12: Army announces it is investigating charges that Lt. William Calley shot more than 100 civilians at My Lai in March 1968.

November 14–15: Largest antiwar demonstration held in Washington.

December 31: U.S. troop strength down to 474,400. U.S. troops killed in combat during 1969 total 9,414.

1970

April 20: President Nixon announces another 150,000 U.S. troops will be withdrawn by spring of 1971.

April 29: U.S. and South Vietnamese troops launch attack against North Vietnamese and Viet Cong sanctuaries across Cambodian border. White House says operation will take six to eight weeks.

May 2: First major bombing raids against North Vietnam since November 1968.

May 2: Demonstrations against Cambodian operation held on college campuses.

May 4: Four students killed by Ohio National Guard soldiers at Kent State University.

May 9: Protests against Cambodian operation held in Washington, New York and other cities. More than 200 colleges closed.

June 24: Senate votes 81 to 10 to repeal 1964 Gulf of Tonkin resolution.

June 29: All U.S. forces withdrawn from Cambodia.

June 30: Senate adopts Cooper-Church amendment barring U.S. military personnel from Cambodia.

October 7: President Nixon makes new five-point peace proposal based on cease-fire in place throughout Indochina.

December 22: Congress gives final approval to Cooper-Church amendment.

December 31: Congress gives final approval to repeal of Gulf of Tonkin resolution.

1971

February 8: South Vietnamese forces enter Laos to attack North Vietnamese supply lines.

April 7: President Nixon says another 100,000 U.S. troops will be withdrawn by end of year.

May 3–5: Mayday demonstrations held in Washington; more than 10,000 arrested.

June 13: The New York Times begins publication of the Pentagon Papers on the war.

December 26–30: American planes stage heavy bombing of military targets in North Vietnam.

1972

January 13: President Nixon announces that U.S. troops will be reduced to 69,000 by May 1.

January 25: President Nixon reveals secret Paris peace talks held by his national security adviser, Henry Kissinger, since August 1969.

March 30: North Vietnamese troops launch spring offensive across DMZ and attack South Vietnamese bases throughout country.

April 16: B52 raids resume around Hanoi and Haiphong.

April 22: Antiwar demonstrators in U.S. cities protest bombings.

May 8: President Nixon orders mining of North Vietnamese harbors.

August 12: Last U.S. ground combat troops leave Vietnam. About 43,500 service personnel, advisers and pilots remain.

October 10: Democratic presidential candidate George McGovern announces plan to end all bombing and withdraw all forces.

October 26: Hanoi Radio announces breakthrough in Paris peace talks. Henry Kissinger says "peace is at hand."

November 1: President Thieu, in radio speech, objects to terms of peace agreement.

November 7: President Nixon is reelected.

November 20: Kissinger and North Vietnamese negotiator Le Duc Tho resume private talks.

December 13: Paris talks end without agreement.

December 18: Full bombing and mining of North Vietnam resumed.

December 30: Bombing halted above 20th parallel. Paris talks scheduled to resume in January.

1973

January 15: White House announces total halt of bombing and mining of North Vietnam based on progress in Paris talks.

January 23: President Nixon announces agreement has been reached for "peace with honor."

January 27: Cease-fire begins.

February 12: First group of American prisoners of war released by North Vietnam and Viet Cong.

March 29: Last group of American POWs flies out of Hanoi. Last American troops leave South Vietnam.

1975

April 30: Saigon is surrendered to Communists. Remaining Americans evacuated.

SUGGESTED ADDITIONAL READING

In addition to the books excerpted in Part One of this volume, a growing body of literature deals with the American involvement in Vietnam. Many of the books published during and immediately after the war were polemics, and are of interest now chiefly as specimens of the intensity of the feelings the war aroused. Many others are primarily for specialists. The brief list that follows, though far from complete, may serve as a starting point for readers who want to learn more about the war and its consequences:

America in Vietnam, by Guenter Lewy (Oxford University Press, 1978) examines the charges against U.S. military policy in the war and finds most of them unjustified. The book is a valuable source of official statistics.

Born on the Fourth of July, by Ron Kovic (McGraw-Hill, 1976) is an angry memoir by a Marine sergeant who comes back from Vietnam paralyzed from the chest down.

Everything We Had, by Al Santoli (Random House, 1981) is an oral history of the war by 33 veterans.

Fire in the Lake, by Frances FitzGerald (Atlantic-Little, Brown, 1972) explains the U.S. failure in Vietnam in terms of the cultural gap between Vietnamese and Americans.

Fire in the Streets, by Milton Viorst (Simon & Schuster, 1979), a history of America in the 1960s, includes several excellent chapters on the antiwar movement.

Friendly Fire, by C.D.B. Bryan (Putnam, 1976) is the story of the radicalization of an Iowa farm couple whose son is killed by an American artillery round.

Nam, by Mark Baker (Morrow, 1981) is another oral history project, this one by about 100 anonymous speakers.

Patriotism Without Flags, by Daniel Lang (Norton, 1974) celebrates the Americans who resisted the war.

Tet! by Don Oberdorfer (Doubleday, 1971) is a vivid account of the 1968 communist offensive and its crucial impact on U.S. public opinion.

The Irony of Vietnam, by Leslie H. Gelb with Richard K. Betts (Brookings Institution, 1979) is an analytical history of U.S. policy-making. Gelb, its principal author, headed the team that compiled the Pentagon Papers.

The Lost Crusade, by Chester L. Cooper (Dodd, Mead, 1970) is an inside account of U.S. policy-making by an official who took part in several efforts to negotiate an end to the war.

The Lost Revolution, by Robert Shaplen (Harper & Row, Colophon paperback, 1966) is a history of American involvement in Vietnam since 1944.

The Making of a Quagmire, by David Halberstam (Random House, 1965) is a reporter's chronicle of American frustration in the 1961–63 Vietnam of Ngo Dinh Diem, culminating in Diem's overthrow.

The Pentagon Papers, The New York Times edition (Quadrangle, 1971), is an abridged version of the official history of the war compiled by the Defense Department.

The Village, by F. J. West Jr. (Harper & Row, 1972) is a Marine captain's report on 17 months in the life of a village in Quang Ngai Province.

The Village of Ben Suc, by Jonathan Schell (Knopf, 1967) is the story of an attack on a communist-controlled village near Saigon.

The War at Home, by Thomas Powers (Grossman, 1973) is the fullest account so far of the antiwar movement.

To What End, by Ward Just (Houghton Mifflin, 1968) is an impressionistic cross-section of the war as the American escalation was reaching its peak.

Tonkin Gulf, by Eugene G. Windchy (Doubleday, 1971) and *Truth Is the First Casualty,* by Joseph C. Goulden (Rand McNally, 1969), both examine the 1964 naval incident that led to congressional authorization of the war.

Yale Studies in English, 191